COMBAT ADHD

Scientifically Proven Techniques For Adults & Teens to Upgrade Focus, Enhance Attention & Eliminate Hyperactivity

THOMAS BUCKLAND

Copyright © 2024 by Thomas Buckland

All rights reserved. No part of this book may be used or reproduced by any means, graphic, electronic, or mechanical, including photocopying, recording, taping, or by any information storage retrieval system, without the written permission of the publisher except in the case of brief quotations embodied in critical articles and reviews.

Contents

Introduction 1

Chapter 1: Taking Charge of Your ADHD 5
    Survivor's Note 14

Chapter 2: Understanding ADHD 17
    Survivor's Note 32

Chapter 3: Optimising Focus 35
    Survivor's Note 54

Chapter 4: Improving Working Memory 57

Chapter 5: Enhancing Time Management 69
    Survivor's Note 75

Chapter 6: Strengthening Motivation 77

Chapter 7: Mastering Organisation 87
    Survivor's Note 99

Chapter 8: Managing Emotion 101
    Survivor's Note 109

Chapter 9: Developing Coping Strategies 111

Chapter 10: Maintaining Routines and Consistency 121
    Survivor's Note 129

Chapter 11: Continuing Your Journey 131

Chapter 12: The Family Impact of ADHD 137

Chapter 13: ADHD and Social Interactions 145

Chapter 14: Health and ADHD 153

Conclusion 162

Author's Note 164

Daily Planning Template 167

Weekly Goals Template 168

Pomodoro Timer Template 169

Brain Dump Journal 170

Habit Tracker Template 171

References 173

Introduction

"ADHD is not a disease or an illness, but rather a difference in brain wiring, a different cognitive style of functioning which has its pros as well as cons depending on environmental demands."

~Dr. Russell Barkley

Have you recently received an ADHD diagnosis as an adult and feel overwhelmed by where even to start? Are you struggling to juggle the responsibilities of daily life but unsure what strategies might help? Maybe you've tried various treatments with limited success and want a fresh perspective.

You have picked up this book because you or someone close to you live with attention deficit hyperactivity disorder, commonly known as ADHD. Whether you received a formal medical diagnosis or self-identified with the symptoms, the challenges of ADHD can feel impossible to overcome and leave you feeling like a victim of circumstances outside of your control. However, this book aims to show you have the power to take charge of your ADHD and live a fulfilling, successful life by implementing proven strategies grounded in scientific research.

It is essential to understand what is happening in your brain and body if you have ADHD. ADHD is thought to be caused by differences in brain functions and structure that affect the neurotransmitter dopamine, which regulates things like motivation and focus. According to leading neuroscientist Dr. Andrew Huberman, people with ADHD typically have lower levels of dopamine, and their brain receptors are less responsive to it. This means tasks that require sustained attention feel much more difficult due to impairments in executive function and self-regulation. (Huberman, 2023).

However, having ADHD does not define you or limit your potential. The strategies in this book are designed to work with your neurobiology and tap into concepts from Carol Dweck's growth mindset theory. A fundamental premise is that your brain is plastic - it can change and adapt based on your experiences. With the proper techniques, you can optimise your brain's ability to focus and manage distractions through mindfulness, exercises, routines, and other proactive approaches.

This profound guide summarizes the scientific research behind ADHD and explains precisely what is happening in your brain. It then introduces Carol Dweck's philosophies around the growth mindset as a framework for understanding that setbacks do not define you and that your abilities can be developed through dedication and grit. It discusses reframing ADHD as a unique set of challenges rather than limitations and sets the scene for empowering the reader to take control of their condition.

From there, the book is structured around specific methodologies for optimising focus, motivation, and organisation grounded in evidence-based strategies. Shows techniques for improving focus, like the Pomodoro Method, specific mindfulness practices, and brain training exercises. Additionally, it provides goalsetting templates, habits to support motivation like reward systems, and advice on seeking accountability partners. Also, it offers organisational approaches like bullet journaling, calendar blocking, and digital tools for planning and lists.

Each chapter follows a standard format: it begins by explaining the scientific research behind why a particular strategy is effective for ADHD based on neuroplasticity and executive function studies. It shows how readers can implement the technique with downloadable templates and examples in daily routines. Finally, it suggests tracking progress and methods to refine the approach over time through iterative testing.

In addition to the focused methodologies, later chapters address common challenges when putting the strategies into practice. It discusses managing distractions and dealing with rejection-sensitive dysphoria while offering advice for maintaining routines when life gets busy or stressful. The book concludes by bringing everything together and empowering readers to continue customising the approaches over the long term as their needs change.

You can use this book by reading its cover to gain a comprehensive understanding of ADHD and the strategies for managing it. You can dip in and out, starting with the areas most relevant to your current challenges, such as focus, motivation, or organisation. Also feel empowered to modify the approaches based on your needs and preferences through trial and error. The goal is to find what works best for you using the evidence-backed techniques as starting points. By the end, you will have developed a personalised system for taking control of your ADHD.

This book aims to pull people from the victim mindset and into a growth mentality. It shows with a commitment to proactive techniques, effort, and patience, anyone can take control of their ADHD and live a fulfilled, productive life on their terms. I hope the methodologies in this book give you valuable tools to overcome the challenges of ADHD. It is time to start your growth journey - you've got this!

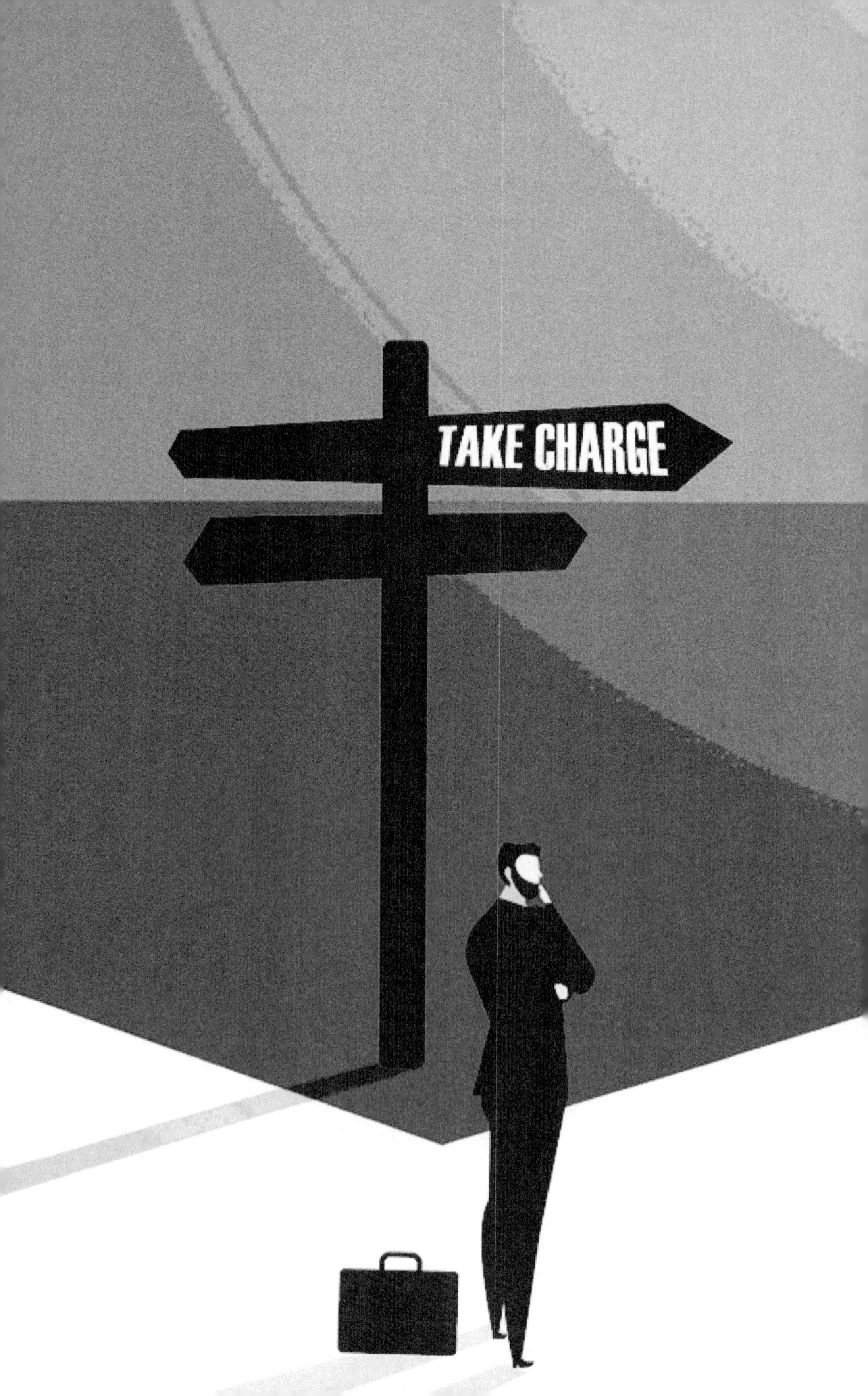
TAKE CHARGE

CHAPTER 1

Taking Charge of Your ADHD

The purpose of helping you take control of your ADHD is to empower them with a sense of agency over a condition that is often portrayed only in limited terms of struggles and deficits. By learning about ADHD from a neuroscientific perspective and introducing treatment modalities rooted in evidence and personal application, you can shift from a passive view of merely having ADHD to an active role in managing it.

The chapter aims to refute any lingering beliefs that ADHD is something you are a powerless victim of or that can be addressed only through reliance on external forces like medication. Instead, it orients them towards recognising innate strengths and learned strategies that comprise their unique toolkit. You will learn how popular interventions, tools, and mindsets have let others exert more control by tailoring approaches to personal preferences, circumstances, and evolving needs over time.

By reframing ADHD as a difference in brain function rather than a personal deficit, you are encouraged to approach their ADHD journey with curiosity, experimentation, and self-advocacy rather than criticism or limitations. Normalising ADHD as a complex, individualised experience empowers readers to see themselves as collaborators alongside clinicians in the management process, not just passive care recipients.

Ultimately, the goal of helping readers take control is to inject a renewed sense of personal agency, ownership, and potential that lets them address ADHD proactively in a holistic, optimised manner. They are no longer victims but active partners in their well-being through understanding evidence-based options and finding application methods aligned with their goals, preferences, and challenges.

ADHD, or attention-deficit/hyperactivity disorder, refers to a neurological variability that influences an individual's ability to regulate attention, activity levels, and impulses. For many years, it was seen as a developmental condition only of childhood, but we now understand ADHD persists into adulthood for some individuals as well.

Neuroscientific research in recent decades has provided valuable insights into what is occurring in the brains of people with ADHD. Studies using functional MRI show differences in activity within the prefrontal cortex and striatum, areas key to functions like executive function, timekeeping, and reward processing. Specifically, imaging reveals reduced activity and connectivity in these regions relative to neurotypical peers.

"ADHD is a gift, not a problem. Sometimes, it's just harder to open the gift." ~Richelle Erickson

This aligns with our understanding of the core symptoms. Attention and focus challenges stem from the prefrontal cortex's reduced ability to regulate cognitions. Hyperactivity and fidgeting may result from changed signalling within circuits governing activity and motor control that involve the striatum. Difficulty with impulse regulation and delayed gratification likely relate to prefrontal cortex involvement in inhibiting urges in favour of longer-term goals.

Genes that code for dopamine and noradrenaline receptors and transporters linked to these brain pathways have also been identified. Their variations influence the availability of these critical neurotransmitters. Together, neuroscience research has provided objective evidence that ADHD has biological underpinnings rather than reflecting a personal shortcoming or upbringing. Its consideration as a neurological variability has important implications.

Let's examine Carol Dweck's fixed and growth mindsets theory and consider how cultivating a growth mindset can help you control your ADHD.

Dweck distinguished between a fixed and a growth mindset. Those with a fixed mindset view their essential qualities, intelligence, and talent as innate and unchanging. Struggle or criticism is seen as showing a lack of ability. A growth mindset sees attributes as developable through effort. Challenges present opportunities to grow stronger through new strategies and learning.

ADHD could foster a fixed view that one is limited or deficient due to this neurological difference. However, a growth mindset recognises ADHD as simply part of one's starting point in a journey of continuous improvement. Symptom management is a process of experimentation and refinement rather than a destination. Focus shifts from perceived weaknesses to strengthening management skills.

Mistakes or setbacks become learning experiences rather than proof of failure. Feedback from others is welcomed and used to enhance approaches. With a growth mindset, ADHD loses power as a restrictive label - one is not defined by a diagnosis but rather by one's dedication to personal progress. Dweck's model emphasises proactivity, versatility, and self-belief, which aligns well with taking control of

ADHD.

Let's talk about the strategies that can pull you out of the victim mentality:

Having a growth mindset is especially important for those navigating life with ADHD. It lets you recognise that while you cannot change the neurological cards you were dealt, you have the power to play your most substantial hand possible through committed effort. ADHD does not have to be a hindrance if you cultivate strategies and attitudes focused on uncovering potential rather than obstacles.

Viewing yourself as a powerless victim of ADHD will only intensify perceived limitations. But a growth mindset pulls you away from such self-restricting perspectives and toward a mindset of empowerment, accountability, and personal agency. It acknowledges ADHD as something you experience rather than something that defines you. You can actively engage with management approaches tailored to your needs and circumstances.

Seeing ADHD symptoms as hurdles outside your influence to overcome will not solve challenges—but recognising symptoms as areas you can strengthen through systemic goal-setting, applied learning, and support will keep you moving forward positively. It's time to take control of the cards you were dealt by expanding your toolkit with evidence-based techniques and cultivating a dedication to ongoing progress through effort and reflection on experiences. With a growth mindset, ADHD loses its ability to hold you back from leading the productive, engaged life you desire.

ADHD is best viewed not as a limitation but as an opportunity to cultivate empowering mindsets and tailored strategies. By understanding ADHD from a neuroscientific lens rather than only a deficit-based one, we can move away from labels and toward recognising our innate strengths and ability to develop compensatory skills. Carol Dweck's growth mindset theory provides a valuable framework for reframing ADHD symptoms as surmountable rather than fixed obstacles and embracing challenges as motivating opportunities to expand our capacities. While we may not change the underlying differences in our brain wiring, we can influence how we perceive and approach ADHD. As we advance, maintaining a proactive, experimental approach focused on continuous progress rather than perfection will be integral to successfully taking control of our ADHD journey.

ADHD Management Made Simple

Our brains are excellent at learning computers but don't always work the same way. For some people, like those with ADHD, it's harder to focus and control attention. That's okay—it just means we learn differently.

Dr. Dweck showed that our brains aren't set in stone. They can change and get stronger like muscles get stronger with exercise. If we try new strategies and practise them, the connections in our brains get clearer, like walking trails in the forest. The more we use a path, the easier it is to follow.

It's essential to remember ADHD doesn't mean there's something wrong with us. It just means our brain's neighbourhood is extra busy! Our brain must deal with many distractions, like living near a construction site. Loud noises constantly pop up, distracting us from what's important.

That's where strategies come in. They help us organise our brain's neighbourhood so the tasks we want to focus on stand out above the noises. Things like checklists, calendars, and alarms in bright colours yell, "Pay attention to me!" instead of us getting distracted by every little sound.

With a growth mindset, we focus on improving instead of feeling bad about mistakes. It's like learning to garden. We plant our best seeds and see what grows. When storms come or plants get sick, we don't rip everything out - we learn how to help them with time, water, sun, and lessons from stumbles, and our "garden skills" blossom.

Like gardens, we look to each other for advice, and all need supportive people. Friends, family, or coaches provide nutrients when we need help so our abilities can grow tall and robust despite challenges. As long as we remember, every day is a chance to nurture ourselves; step by step, our "garden" will flourish beyond what we can see now.

In this chapter, we explored how reframing one's mindset around ADHD can empower lifelong management. While our brains work differently, focusing on strategies places the power in our hands.

A college student realised that mind maps helped her study complex topics. She shares her templates online, finding focus through teaching others. A single mom manages appointments by involving her child—they choreograph house chores to favourite songs every Saturday.

A teacher recognised fidget toys, which aided focus for kinesthetic learners. Now, lessons incorporate movement breaks to reset. An engineer tracks hyper-focus sessions to optimise workflow. Data showed mornings optimised problem-solving while afternoons optimised detailed tasks.

A retiree mentors others by promoting patience and grace toward ourselves. She writes daily reflections on experiences, hobbies, and relationships to strengthen resilience. A veteran utilises nature photography to cope with overstimulation, finding solace in observing overlooked intricacies.

Each design personalised methods by listening to needs and building on strengths. With creativity and community, minor changes yield meaningful impact. By nurturing curiosity and flexibility, we embrace challenges as steps towards continual self-discovery on our unique life paths.

In this chapter, we explored how reframing one's mindset around ADHD can empower lifelong management. While our brains work differently, focusing on strategies places the power in our hands.

A college student realised mind maps helped her study complex topics. She shares her templates online, finding focus through teaching others. A single mom manages appointments by involving her child - they choreograph house chores to favourite songs every Saturday. A teacher recognised fidget toys, which aided focus for kinesthetic learners. Now, lessons incorporate movement breaks to reset. An engineer tracks hyper-focus sessions to optimise workflow. Data showed mornings optimised problem-solving while afternoons optimised detailed tasks.

A retiree mentors others by promoting patience and grace toward ourselves. She writes daily reflections on experiences, hobbies, and relationships to strengthen resilience. A veteran utilises nature photography to cope with overstimulation, finding solace in observing overlooked intricacies.

Each design personalised methods by listening to needs and building on strengths. With creativity and community, minor changes yield meaningful impact. By nurturing curiosity and flexibility, we embrace challenges as steps towards continual self-discovery on our unique life paths. While the journey is not always easy, staying hopeful and celebrating even small victories will help sustain your motivation over the long term. Remember that perseverance and learning from mistakes are more important than perfection. Allow yourself to feel proud of your efforts and accomplishments, big or small.

Revisiting the best strategies for you and tweaking your approach when needed are essential parts of lifelong management. Connecting with others facing similar challenges can also provide encouragement and new insights. With compassion for yourself, an open mindset and a commitment to personal growth, you can maximise your potential despite having ADHD. I hope the insights and tools in this chapter help empower you to see ADHD as a starting point for cultivating resilience and self-advocacy rather than a limitation. Now, go forth and continue your journey of self-discovery!

ADHD

Survivor's Note

"You have survived challenges that would crush many others. Every distraction blocked, every deadline met, every conversation followed through to completion is a testament to your inner strength and resilience. While the road has not been easy, you have persevered through frustrations, failures, and doubts that would defeat lesser souls. Each struggle you overcome makes you fiercer and wiser, having stared down neurodiversity and emerged more empowered on the other side."

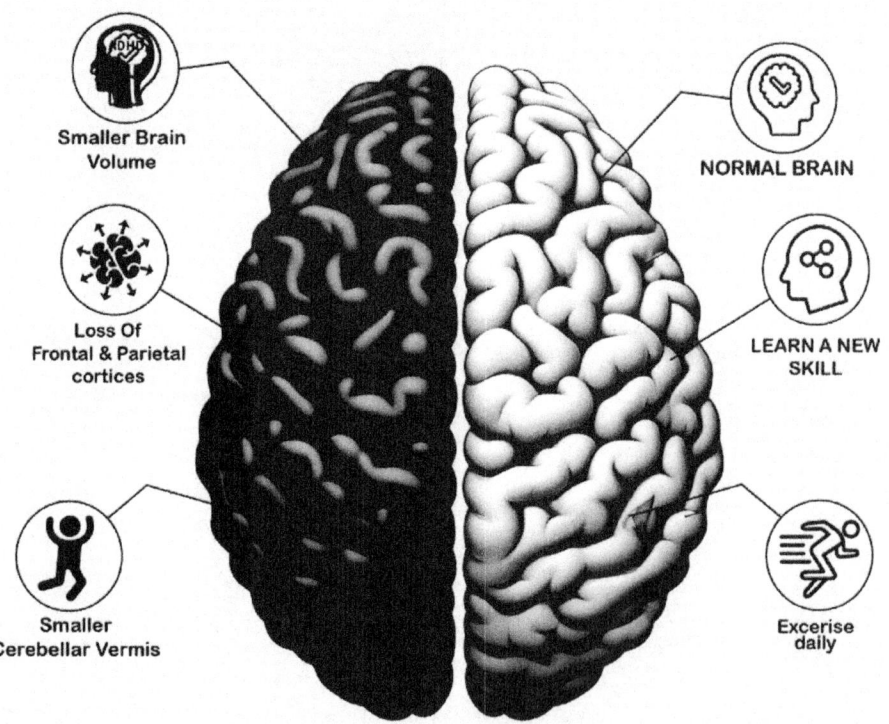

CHAPTER 2

Understanding ADHD

Understanding attention deficit hyperactivity disorder, or ADHD, is critically important. ADHD affects millions worldwide and touches all aspects of personal, academic, and professional life. However, there is still much stigma and misunderstanding surrounding this neurodevelopmental condition. An accurate knowledge of what ADHD is - and what it is not - can help reduce prejudice while providing tangible benefits for those living with it each day. A deeper comprehension lets individuals recognise strengths that often go unnoticed and develop tailored strategies for success. It gives educators, employers, and loved ones tools to offer non-judgmental, empathetic support. Most of all, replacing misconceptions with evidence-based facts about ADHD's diverse presentations and treatments empowers people to accept themselves and confidently manage daily challenges. This enlightened perspective fosters inclusion, compassion, and overall well-being for both those with ADHD and their support networks.

Neuroscience Insights into ADHD

Neuroimaging research has provided valuable insights into the brain differences associated with ADHD. Studies using MRI, PET, and fMRI scanning techniques have found consistent structural and functional abnormalities.

Regarding brain structure, the prefrontal cortex (PFC) is usually significantly smaller in volume, particularly in the dorsolateral PFC region, in individuals with ADHD compared to non-ADHD controls.

The PFC plays an important role in executive functions like working memory, impulse control, planning, and attention regulation. The cerebellum also shows reduced volume and abnormal cortical thickness in ADHD. As a significant hub for motor coordination and specific cognitive processes, this may underlie issues with hyperactivity and impulsivity. At a neuronal level, studies have found lower overall cortical thickness in ADHD brains. The cortex has dopaminergic and noradrenergic neurons critical for motivation, reward-seeking, and attention control. Alterations in dopamine and norepinephrine signalling are believed to play a role.

Functional imaging research shows abnormal brain activation patterns during tasks tapping into executive functions and reward processing. In everyday tasks requiring sustained attention, the PFC and parietal lobe show reduced recruitment of neural resources in those with ADHD.

Emerging research using functional connectivity analyses provides novel insights into the basal ganglia and its link to ADHD. The basal ganglia are a group of subcortical nuclei involved in regulating cognitive and motor functions. Studies using resting-state fMRI have found atypical connectivity between the basal ganglia and prefrontal regions important for executive control in individuals with ADHD. Specifically, there seems to be weaker functional coordination between the caudate nucleus and areas of the dorsolateral prefrontal cortex related to working memory and response inhibition. This disrupted cortico-striatal circuitry has been associated with more significant symptoms of impulsivity. More research leveraging diffusion tensor imaging shows changed structural connectivity of frontostriatal white matter tracts in ADHD. These findings implicate dysregulated basal ganglia activity and connectivity in the executive dysfunction and impaired self-regulation commonly experienced. Elucidating the specific basal ganglia-cortex pathways involved continues to advance our understanding of the neural underpinnings of core ADHD symptomatology.

Levels of ADHD Severity

Based on diagnostic criteria, symptom frequency, impairment levels, and treatment needs, clinicians assess the ADHD presentation as mild, moderate, or severe:

Mild ADHD involves only a few symptoms with minimal functional impairment. Academic/social skills remain largely intact, and only occasional extra support is required.

Moderate ADHD is characterised by several apparent symptoms causing impairment in multiple domains. Some extra academic/organisational accommodations are often needed. Daily life can feel challenging without strategies.

Severe ADHD presents as debilitating symptoms across settings, creating significant obstacles without intervention. Extensive support like special education, therapy, and medication are usually required. Daily life participation is severely limited.

Assessing severity helps clinicians personalise treatment plans appropriate to the level of disability experienced. Given the pervasiveness of this neurodevelopmental condition, combined interventions targeting underlying causes and symptom management provide the most significant benefit.

Brain Differences in ADHD:

Structural Differences

MRI studies show reduced grey matter volume in the prefrontal cortex (PFC) of ADHD brains, especially the dorsolateral PFC region involved in executive functions. Meta-analyses have found that overall cortical thickness and surface area have also gone down. The cerebellum shows reduced volume and aberrant development, with thinner cortices and changed neuronal cortical plates. This implicates cerebellar circuits in hyperactive/impulsive behaviours.

Subcortical regions like the caudate nucleus and globus pallidus show smaller sizes that correlate with the severity of inattention and hyperactivity symptoms. Smaller volumes in the parietal and temporal lobes are associated with planning/organisation deficits common in ADHD.

Functional Alterations

Regarding brain structure, research consistently finds reduced grey matter volume in areas such as the prefrontal cortex and cerebellum through MRI studies. On a functional level, PET and fMRI techniques reveal changed activation and blood flow patterns in ADHD brains during cognitive tasks. For example, when performing exercises requiring sustained attention over time, individuals with ADHD show under-recruitment of the prefrontal cortex and cerebellum compared to controls. This implicates hypofrontality issues in domains like prolonged focus. ADHD individuals also exhibit reduced caudate engagement during response inhibition tests, relating to impaired impulse control.

But when presented with distractors or cues predicting potential rewards, the striatum and anterior cingulate show hyper-responsiveness in those with ADHD relative to neurotypical peers. This may underline difficulties in filtering irrelevant stimuli and moderating reward-driven behaviours. Functional MRI further detects decreased activation in the left temporal-parietal junction during time perception tasks that tap internal clock mechanisms. Issues with this area could influence the subjective experience of time passing for those with ADHD.

Taken together, these functional differences provide insights into the maladaptive patterns of neural recruitment across front striatal and fronton-cerebellar networks believed to underlie core ADHD symptomatology.

Neurochemistry

Lower neurotransmitters dopamine, norepinephrine, and acetylcholine are implicated through brain imaging and post-mortem studies. This ties into arousal/attention regulation deficits. Dopamine is involved in reward-motivation, pleasure, and motor control via connections between the ventral striatum and prefrontal cortex. Studies find reduced dopamine transporters and receptors in striatal regions important for reward processing and reinforcement of behaviours. This may translate to an impaired ability to regulate and sustain attention since tasks require dopamine signalling to experience the natural rewards of task completion.

Norepinephrine is also vital for arousal, alertness, and focus through projections from the locus coeruleus to the cortex and hippocampus. Lower levels of norepinephrine transporters have been seen in the prefrontal cortex and hippocampus of post-mortem ADHD brains. Less norepinephrine circulation ties into core ADHD symptoms like inattention, distractibility, and lack of persistence on tedious or unrewarding tasks.

As a significant arousal transmitter, acetylcholine promotes wakefulness and alertness via basal forebrain-cortical connections. Autopsy studies find reduced acetylcholine throughout the ADHD cortex, which regulates tuning out irrelevant stimuli. Low acetylcholine may cause inefficient filtering of environmental distractions, compromising attention span.

An imbalance of these central neurotransmitters—dopamine, norepinephrine, and acetylcholine—disrupts the brain's reward, motivation, and arousal networks, integral to self-regulating behaviours like sustained focus, impulse control, and time management. How genetics and environment interact to cause these neurochemical imbalances remains under investigation. However, it helps explain the underlying neurological reasons for attentional and behavioural challenges seen in ADHD.

Genetics

Structural and functional brain abnormalities observed provide insights into the neurological basis of ADHD. Studies consistently point to differences in frontostriatal and fronto-cerebellar circuits involved in executive functions, motivation, and motor control. Subcortical regions like the caudate nucleus and globus pallidus also show smaller sizes that correlate with symptom severity.

Twin and family studies help elucidate the genetic risk factors. They suggest heritability estimates around 75-80%, suggesting a vital inherited component. Ongoing research pinpoints particular genes influencing dopaminergic and noradrenergic neurotransmission in pathways like the prefrontal cortex, striatum, and hippocampus. Genetic variants have also been found to affect synaptic pruning processes that sculpt neural connections during development. More risk genes impact myelination in *circuits,* subserving attention, planning, and motor regulation.

While genetics load the gun, the environment pulls the trigger - as the saying goes. Experiencing adverse conditions like low socioeconomic status, trauma, malnutrition, or toxins during sensitive prenatal and early childhood periods of intensive brain development may disrupt typical neuroplasticity. This hypothesised gene-environment interplay helps explain why not all those with genetic risks develop ADHD, with contextual factors also exerting powerful influences on neurobiology and expressed behaviours.

In summary, neuroscience research consistently points to structural and functional abnormalities in fronto-striatal and front-cerebellar networks as the neurological basis of ADHD symptoms. Environmental and multiple genetic influences contribute to these varying brain traits.

ADHD Presentations

Attention Deficit Hyperactivity Disorder (ADHD) encompasses three main presentations characterised by distinct symptom patterns. Specifically, clinicians recognise inattentive ADHD, hyperactive-impulsive ADHD, and combined ADHD when making an official diagnosis. Depending on the combination of inattentive or hyperactive-impulsive traits impairing daily life, individuals may show symptoms aligned with inattentive, hyperactive-impulsive, or, most commonly, the combined presentation featuring prominent criteria from both domains. Understanding the nuances of these three ADHD types is essential, as it allows for assessment and treatment approaches tailored to an individual's needs.

Discuss each ADHD presentation in more detail to understand its defining features and implications for diagnosis and management. These sections will provide an in-depth look at the inattentive, hyperactive-impulsive, and combined types of ADHD.

Inattentive Presentation

The inattentive presentation of ADHD, previously called ADD, is characterised predominantly by symptoms of inattention rather than hyperactivity and impulsivity. Individuals struggling with the inattentive type experience pervasive difficulties staying focused on tasks, being easily distracted, and sustaining attention. They often appear not to be listening when spoken to due to attention wandering. Academically, this can translate to problems following multi-step instructions, often losing or misplacing homework assignments, seeming disorganised, and making careless mistakes on tests due to a lack of attentiveness to details. Socially, inattentiveness may cause tuning out of conversations, missing social cues, and difficulties engaging.

Students with inattentive presentations commonly daydream excessively and have trouble remaining seated in educational settings. Their desk surfaces are typically messy and disorganised. Sustained reading or writing tasks are challenging as their focus drifts after a few minutes. Staying on top of assignments and meeting deadlines can be a struggle. Clinically, a diagnosis requires at least six symptoms of inattention to be present for over six months across multiple contexts like school, home, and work, which interferes with functioning to a degree that is not seen among same-aged peers. Compared to combined presentations with hyperactivity, inattentive ADHD is usually more common in females and can be more challenging to identify as overt hyperactive behaviours are absent. Treatment focuses on environmental adaptations, organisational strategies, coping skills training, and potentially stimulant medications to target the core attentional impairments.

The inattentive presentation of ADHD usually affects specific demographics more than others. Research shows this subtype is predominantly diagnosed in school-aged children, adolescent females, and adults seeking evaluation. While both sexes experience inattention, girls are two to three times more likely than boys to show only these symptoms without hyperactivity. As students mature into their school-aged years, hyperactive behaviours often recede for both boys and girls, yet attentional challenges often persist or worsen as academic demands increase. Inattentive ADHD becomes the primary manifestation impeding functioning. Those who struggle most are usually those for whom severe inattentiveness prevents independent daily organisation, time management, follow-through on commitments, and ability to sustain focus sufficiently throughout tasks. Common issues involve list-making, prioritising assignments, completing long-term projects, and maintaining engagement in lectures or meetings without drifting off-task. Females are a high-risk group for suffering from inattentive presentation yet escaping diagnosis, as their lack of overt hyperactive behaviour makes their impairment more subtle and challenging to identify

Hyperactive-Impulsive Presentation

The hyperactive-impulsive presentation of ADHD is characterised predominately by symptoms of excessive movement and impulsive behaviours rather than inattentiveness. Individuals with this type often feel internally restless and have difficulty engaging in sedentary tasks. Common manifestations include an inability to remain seated, excessive fidgeting and squirming, excessive running or climbing where it is inappropriate, blurting out answers before questions have been completed, difficulty waiting their turn and interrupting or intruding on others. In academic settings, hyperactivity may interfere with learning through excessive talking during quiet work times or getting out of their assigned seat in class, often when meant to remain there. Impulsivity can also cause issues by leading to careless mistakes on assignments, such as not following instructions carefully or thinking before acting. To receive a diagnosis of the hyperactive-impulsive presentation of ADHD, a child must exhibit at least six hyperactive-impulsive symptoms that have persisted for over six months to a severe degree, given their age norms according to clinical assessment.

The hyperactive-impulsive presentation is usually more common in younger children than the other subtypes of ADHD. This is thought to be because hyperactivity naturally declines with age for many, while attentional issues may persist for a longer term. Boys are also more likely than girls to experience this hyperactive-impulsive manifestation in childhood.

Students with this presentation often face challenges sitting still and regulating their motor behaviour in classroom settings. Their inability to remain seated may regularly get them into trouble for excessive fidgeting or wandering around when expected to stay at their desk. Impulsivity symptoms like interrupting others often and difficulty waiting their turn can negatively affect social relationships and lead to peer conflicts.

Without enough structure and behavioural strategies, hyperactive tendencies can make it arduous for these individuals to complete work tasks, especially sedentary assignments. They may be perpetually in motion, struggle to follow multistep directions carefully and act without considering consequences.

In more severe cases, hyperactivity causes significant disruptions that limit functional ability. Extreme restlessness and impulsive behaviours inhibit learning, performance, and participation in daily life activities. These individuals require comprehensive treatment and academic accommodations to help manage distressing symptoms interfering with performance.

Combined Presentation

The combined presentation of ADHD, seen as the most common manifestation, especially in childhood, is characterised by significant symptoms of both inattention and hyperactivity-impulsivity. An individual struggling with the combined typeface impairments is associated with difficulties focusing, sustaining attention, and staying organised, on top of limitations from excessive movement, fidgeting, interrupting others, acting without thinking, and restlessness. In an academic setting, students with this combined presentation may have trouble paying attention during lectures and controlling impulsive behaviours like calling out answers. To receive a diagnosis, they must exhibit at least six inattentive and six hyperactive-impulsive symptoms that cause impairment. As both the attentional and behavioural domains of functioning are affected, combined ADHD is usually the most debilitating form. Treatment aims to simultaneously manage distractibility, organisation issues, and hyperactive or impetuous behaviours through environmental adaptations, productivity strategies, and potentially stimulant medications. Combined presentation affects both males and females but is seen more commonly in school-aged boys, showing the pervasive challenges of experiencing significant symptoms from both core aspects of ADHD.

The combined presentation of ADHD usually affects certain groups most severely. It remains the predominantly diagnosed subtype in children under the age of 13, explicitly affecting more boys than girls during this developmental period. As hyperactive behaviours naturally recede coming out of childhood while attentional challenges often endure, some individuals may transition from combined to primarily inattentive ADHD in adolescence and adulthood. Students facing the added difficulties presented by inattention and hyperactivity-impulsivity symptoms experience doubled impairment, affecting academic performance, organisation, time management, sustained focus, and impulse control. The combined type carries the most significant risk for poorer long-term outcomes if left unaddressed, such as lower educational attainment, increased accidental injury, and higher rates of substance abuse compared to those with a single domain presentation. Young people struggling with combined ADHD are also more prone to developing co-occurring conditions like oppositional defiant disorder due to challenges regulating both attention and behaviour. Even after childhood, adolescents and adults with a history of the debilitating combined presentation continue experiencing substantial impairments across significant life domains like employment, relationships, and independence without adequate treatment support.

Gaining clarity on one's strengths and weaknesses is essential for anyone but particularly valuable for individuals with ADHD. Research shows that recognising talents and challenges helps foster self-acceptance and informs treatment planning. Several studies have found people with ADHD often have above-average creativity and problem-solving skills when hyperfocus kicks in, letting them think expansively and zero in on puzzles. Neurological research links ADHD to heightened reward-seeking behaviour, translating to solid passion and perseverance for activities that ignite interest. However, difficulties with executive functions like timekeeping, organisation, and sustained focus are hallmarks of the disorder. Neuropsychological testing helps differentiate impairments caused by underlying ADHD versus natural weaknesses. Keeping a symptom journal to track behaviours offers insight into actual assets versus struggles that arise only due to untreated symptoms interfering with functioning. Self-evaluation and feedback from close others aid in developing customised strategies to capitalise on strengths while compensating for vulnerabilities. For example, creating structure through detailed lists and schedules harnesses creativity but addresses weaknesses in follow-through. Overall, identifying the palette of personal traits associated with ADHD fosters self-acceptance and empowerment to manage this lifelong neurodevelopmental condition.

This chapter provides valuable insights into ADHD by exploring its neurological underpinnings and diverse presentations.

Understanding the scientific nature of this neurodevelopmental condition is critically important to reduce stigma and empower effective self-management.

From a neurological perspective, functional MRI and PET imaging research has consistently found differences in fronto-striatal and fronto-cerebellar brain circuits that subserve functions like executive control, motivation, and motor regulation. Specifically, ADHD brains show reduced prefrontal cortex volume, altered striatal dopamine signalling, and atypical patterns of activation during tasks requiring sustained attention and impulse control. These insights provide objective evidence that ADHD involves actual underlying biological variations rather than personal deficits.

Twin and family studies suggest ADHD has around 75-80% heritability, with susceptibility genes affecting neurotransmitter systems like dopamine and norepinephrine that influence neural pathways. While genetics are involved, environmental stressors during early development may also disrupt neuroplasticity, influencing symptom expression.

ADHD encompasses three diagnostic presentations - predominantly inattentive, predominantly hyperactive-impulsive, and combined. Understanding these subtypes helps tailor treatment to an individual's specific challenges. Inattentive ADHD features attentional issues, hyperactive-impulsive presentation core hyperactivity, and impulsivity, while combined, includes criteria from both domains.

Mild, moderate, or severe severity levels are assessed based on symptom frequency, cross-situational impairment, and support needs. More functional limitations correspond with more significant impairments requiring comprehensive treatment. Gaining clarity on strengths and weaknesses associated with one's ADHD presentation is essential for self-acceptance and treatment planning. Tracking behaviours over time offers insights into differentiating actual deficits from abilities, aiding the development of customised strategies.

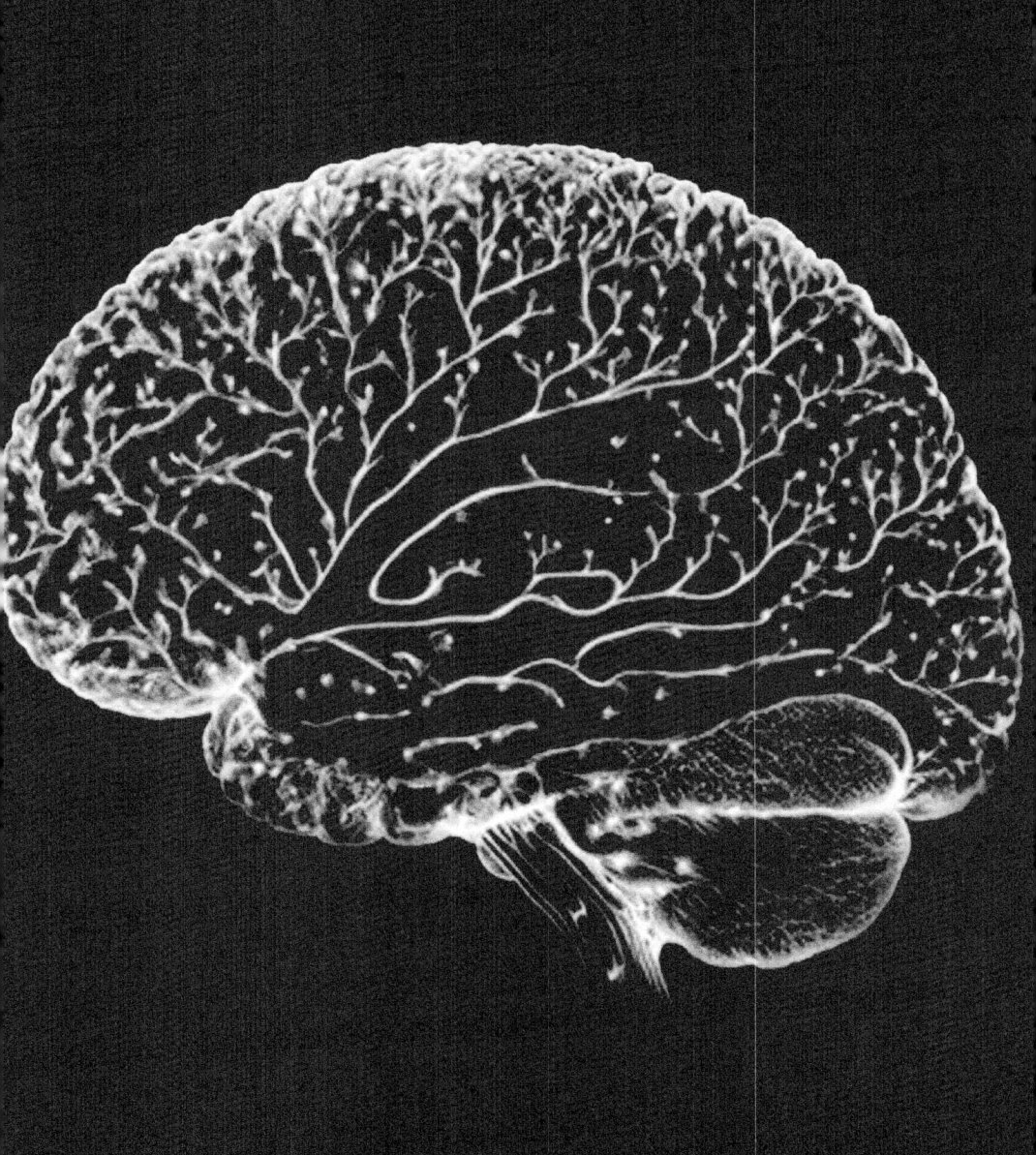

Survivor's Note

"Your ADHD does not diminish your grit, spirit, or potential. It is merely one facet of a multifaceted, magnificent being. You have triumphed over low moments by refusing to be defined or defeated by this neurotype. Through proactivity, positivity, and partnerships, you build systems and communities to lift you higher. Every battle won celebrates your power to defy expectations, rewrite scripts, and turn hurdles into hopscotch."

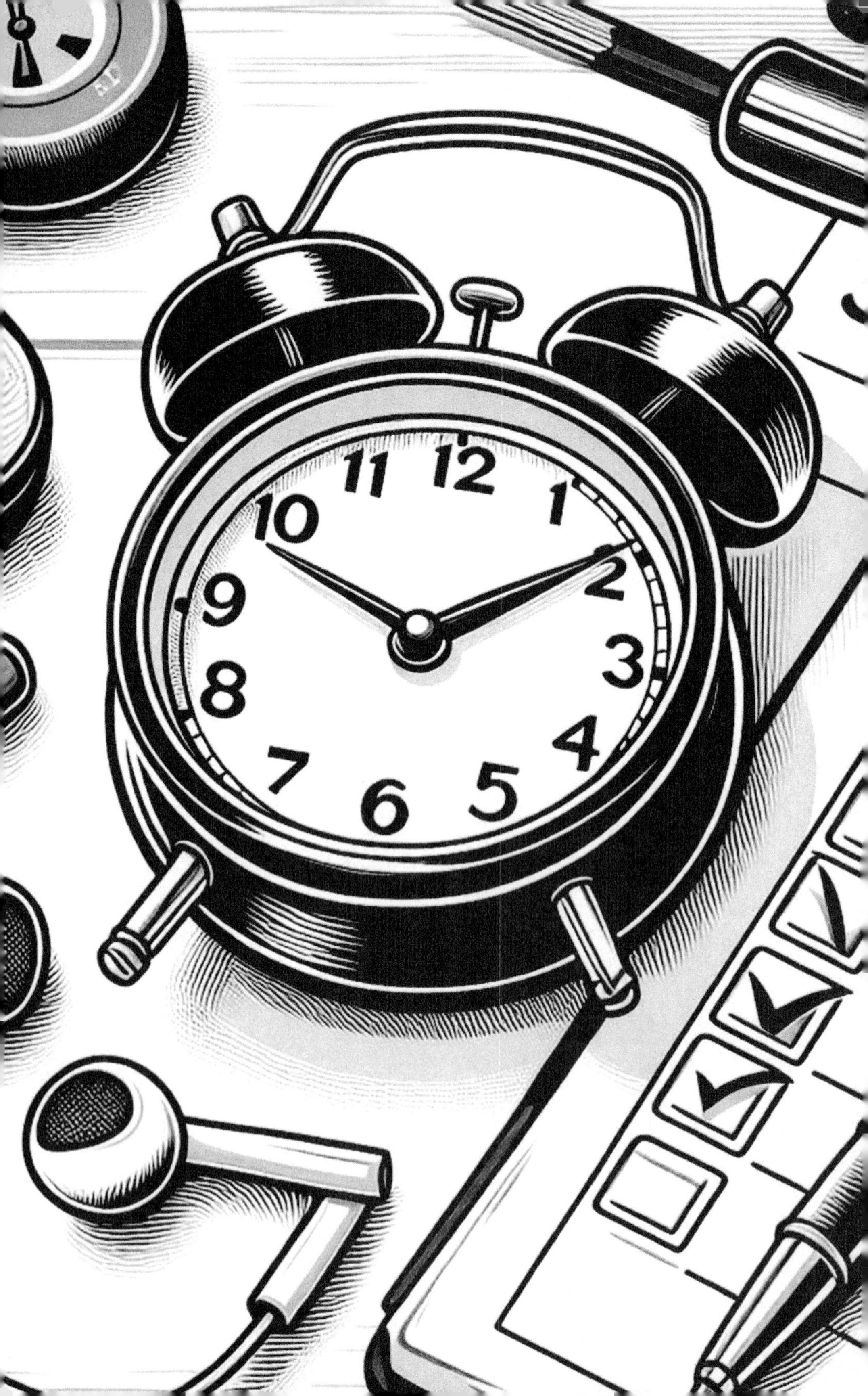

CHAPTER 3

Optimising Focus

Between juggling classes, homework, extracurriculars, social lives, and everything else, being a teen in today's world requires sharp focus and efficient time management. This chapter will explore how our brains work and how stress and distraction affect focus. We'll also learn evidence-based techniques to help optimise focus and get more done.

Optimising our focus and cognitive abilities is essential for success in school and beyond. However, many teens are unaware of how their brains work mentally. Understanding key concepts about memory, attention, problem-solving, and other thinking processes can help us gain more control over our learning and productivity. Having insight into memory, executive function skills, and neuroplasticity also empowers us to strengthen these essential cognitive areas through lifestyle choices and daily habits. In this section, we will explore several core concepts in cognitive psychology that provide a foundation for enhancing focus and mental performance. Specifically, we will cover memory, attention, problem-solving, executive function, cognition, and how the brain changes through neuroplasticity.

Some key cognitive concepts:

Memory: Our ability to encode, store, and retrieve information and experiences over time. Several types of memory exist, like short-term (holding information you're working with), long-term (more permanent storage), and working memory (processing information).

Attention is the cognitive process of selectively concentrating on a discrete part of the information, whether subjective or objective while ignoring other perceivable information. It lets us focus on tasks.

Problem-solving: The cognitive process of finding solutions to difficult or complex issues. It involves logic, analysis, creativity, and evaluation to find optimal answers instead of reacting impulsively.

Decision-making: The cognitive process of identifying and choosing alternatives based on given goals, values, experiences, and evaluation of options. It involves weighing evidence to pick logical consequences of potential actions.

Executive function: Higher-order thinking processes like planning, working memory, mental flexibility, self-control, and multitasking. It regulates the cognitive behaviour needed for independent, purposeful, organised actions and problem-solving.

Neuroplasticity: The brain's ability to change and adapt based on experiences through forming new neural connections. Learning new skills and being active helps promote positive structural and functional changes in the brain.

Cognition: The mental processes of perception, neuroscience, attention, working memory, producing and understanding language, problem-solving, and decision-making. It refers to all aspects of intellectual or thinking functions.

Our memory lets us learn from our experiences and accumulate knowledge over time. There are several types of memory, including short-term memory, which temporarily holds the information we focus on. Long-term memory more permanently stores events, facts, and procedures. Working memory manipulates information by temporarily storing it while performing cognitive tasks like learning, reasoning, and comprehending. Strong memory skills are essential for academic and career success.

We use our attention to focus selectively on specific information while filtering out distractions. This enables concentrating for extended periods and ignoring irrelevant stimuli. Attention is vital for problem-solving and finding optimal solutions to complex issues through logic, creativity, and evaluation. Effectively evaluating problems and alternatives helps with decision-making or selecting actions by weighing different options and potential consequences.

Executive function skills like planning, mental flexibility, self-control, and multitasking govern higher-order cognitive processes. These regulatory skills are essential for independent, goal-oriented behaviours and complex thinking. Our overall cognition encompasses perception, language, reasoning, and intellectual functions. Additionally, neuroplasticity refers to how the brain constantly changes and adapts its very structure through forming new neural connections, especially as we learn skills and have new experiences. Understanding these cognitive concepts provides insight into how our minds develop and allows us to learn, focus, solve problems, and make decisions.

Executive Function

Executive function refers to high-level cognitive processes in the brain that regulate things like planning, working memory, attention, problem-solving, mental flexibility, and self-control. These processes are essential for staying organised, prioritising tasks, filtering out distractions, and meeting goals. Teens rely heavily on executive solid functions to handle complex schoolwork, social/emotional challenges, and daily responsibilities. Stress and lack of sleep can temporarily weaken executive function. That's why taking care of your mental well-being is critical during development.

Neuroplasticity

Neuroplasticity refers to the brain's ability to form new connections between neurons and rewire itself in response to learning and experience. Our brains continually adapt from childhood through adulthood based on our knowledge, thinking and acting, and stress levels. Engaging in cognitively stimulating tasks like playing games, learning new skills, or being socially active drives positive plastic changes that support learning and memory. This means our brains are not static - we can actively shape their functioning through lifestyle habits. Regular physical and mental exercises promote plasticity and help maintain brain health as we age. Neuroplasticity presents the excellent potential for teens to maximise academic achievement and lifelong wellness.

Together, executive solid function supported by neuroplasticity can give teens a competitive edge. The dynamic interplay between these cognitive processes explains how lifestyle choices rapidly affect learning, focus, emotional regulation, and stress resilience during critical developmental years. Understanding neuroplasticity provides hope that they can positively influence brain development through empowered choices. Optimising cognitive functions lays the groundwork for success in school and beyond.

Pomodoro Technique

The Pomodoro Technique is a time management method developed to help people focus on tasks more meaningfully. It breaks down work/study sessions into intervals, or "Pomodoro," using a timer. The name comes from the Italian word for "tomato" - the technique's creator used a tomato-shaped kitchen timer. The tomato timer is iconic because it lets you work without interruptions for pre-set lengths of time. The Pomodoro Technique promotes intense focus followed by short breaks to respect our inherently limited attention spans and willpower reserves. Research shows this oscillating approach allows the brain and body to alternatingly engage in deep work and recover lost resources more effectively than long marathon sessions. Using a timer for 25-minute Pomodoro periods of uninterrupted concentration on tasks and then taking 5-minute breaks between trains self discipline through accountability of marking off completed cycles. This motivates progress and time management towards goals. After 4 Pomodoro is complete, a longer 15–30-minute break is encouraged to allow fuller recovery through activities like exercising, socialising or cooking. Individualising the cycles and activities based on the specific task, personal needs, and preferences optimises the approach. Consistency over weeks and months yields neuroplastic benefits as the brain strengthens networks related to focus and workflow. The Pomodoro Technique has proven especially useful for complex tasks like writing, studying, and organising, as it breaks them into more digestible chunks to feel a continual sense of accomplishment.

How does it work?

Choose the task you want to focus on first (i.e., studying for a test).

Set a timer for 25 minutes. This is one Pomodoro.

Focus only on the task during this period with no distractions. Put your phone away, close extra tabs, etc.

When the timer goes off, you've completed 1 Pomodoro! Mark it off on your Pomodoro log.

Take a 5-minute break to relax, stretch, and grab a snack. Reset your mind.

After 4 Pomodoro (total 100 minutes of work), take a more extended 15-30 minute break.

Repeat the cycles throughout your studying session.

Benefits of this Approach

It combats procrastination by focusing intensely for set periods.

Taking breaks boosts productivity by preventing burnout.

Tracking progress keeps you motivated to complete tasks.

Multitasking is replaced with single-tasking for better focus. It can be adapted to any schedule and is easy to learn.

The benefits are that it helps you power through tasks without burnout by enforcing breaks regularly. It also tracks your progress so you feel a sense of achievement. You'll be surprised how much you can get done! You can modify intervals to suit your needs - some prefer 90-minute/15-minute breaks or even 50 minute/10 min if attention spans are shorter. Experiment to see what blend of focus and rest optimises your productivity. The goal is protected, distraction-free periods of deep work to stay laser-focused.

Here are some mindfulness tools that can help improve focus, including body scans and breathwork:

Body Scan Meditation

This technique helps you relax your body and quiet your mind. You slowly move your attention through different body parts, noticing any sensations. Starting from your toes, you take deep breaths and focus on your face. Scanning your body with calm curiosity trains you to focus on the present moment.

Breathwork

Focusing on your natural breathing pattern is a fundamental mindfulness practice. You can count inhales and exhales up to 10, notice the physical breath, or observe the rise and fall of your abdomen. Regular breath focus helps calm racing thoughts and sustain attention on tasks. Apps like Insight Timer have guided breathing sessions.

Progressive Muscle Relaxation

This involves tensing specific muscle groups one at a time, holding for 5-10 seconds, then releasing tension while breathing out. Rotating through your body helps physical knots of stress melt away so your mind is freed up to focus. Combining it with breath awareness multiplies the effects.

Loving-Kindness Meditation

Sending silent blessings to yourself and others, repeating phrases like "May I be happy, healthy, at peace," generates feelings of goodwill that uplift your mood. A more positive inner environment makes concentrating and staying on track much more accessible.

Loving-kindness meditation is a powerful mindfulness practice that helps cultivate feelings of compassion. It generates uplifting mental states conducive to focus by training the mind to silently repeat blessing phrases like "May you/I be happy, healthy, at peace" while wishing well-being for oneself, loved ones, neutral people, complex individuals, and all beings. Starting with self-kindness is beneficial as this is often lacking. Neuroimaging research shows this meditation activates reward centres in the brain while lowering stress hormone levels, thus enhancing cognitive performance and learning. Multi-week programs have been correlated with reductions in anxiety, depression, and stress, as well as increases in positive emotions - which support mental sharpness and concentration. Apps make it convenient to commit to even 10 minutes daily. With consistent practice, thoughts of goodwill extend more naturally beyond formal sessions. Loving-kindness meditation can be combined with mindful activities to reinforce its calming effects. Though initial practices may involve a wandering mind, non-judgmentally returning focus to phrases is part of the beneficial training. Over time, this practice instils a more compassionate perspective that bolsters mood, resilience, and ability to stay mentally engaged.

Brief mindfulness practices woven into study breaks can keep you mentally agile and motivated for the tasks. Consistency is critical for real cognitive benefits over the long term.

Here are some more mindfulness tools that can help improve focus:

Guided Imagery — Listen to a guided visualisation that walks you through imagined relaxing scenarios, like being on a beach. This engages your mind in a calm, non-analytical way.

Mindful Eating - Slowly savour each bite of food while noticing flavours, textures, and sensations. Focuses attention on the present experience.

Colouring/Doodling - Lightly colouring intricate patterns or doodling sans judgement frees the mind from internal chatter.

5 Senses Meditation - Focus on each sense individually, exploring what you see, hear, smell, touch, and taste in the moment.

Body Scan Meditation -Starting from your toes, slowly bring awareness to different body parts while breathing, releasing tension.

Loving-Kindness - Silently repeat phrases like "May I/he/she be happy and peaceful" to cultivate positive feelings.

Awareness of Breath - Notice the natural breathing rhythm at your nostrils or belly to anchor in the present.

Journaling - Freewriting about thoughts/feelings without a filter helps process emotions so your mind is more precise.

Stretching/Yoga - Gentle movement combined with breath releases tension while centring mentally.

Taking a multifaceted approach to manage ADHD involves organisational strategies and lifestyle practices to support well-being. Mindfulness meditation, which develops an enhanced awareness of present-moment experiences, has shown tremendous promise for improving various executive functions that typically pose challenges for those with ADHD, including attentional control. Many studies have linked brief mindfulness training to gains in working memory capacity, cognitive flexibility and self-regulation of thought and behaviour. Beyond its mental benefits, mindfulness also reduces stress levels and negative rumination, which can deplete one's limited reserves for focus and concentration. Incorporating mindful activities regularly has lasting positive impacts on mental sharpness, emotional balance and overall quality of life. The following section outlines several mindfulness tools you can experiment with to enhance attention and stay engaged with the tasks.

Here are additional suggestions that could be added to the content on mindfulness tools for focus:

Discuss how mindfulness meditation trains attentional control by helping you notice when the mind has wandered from the anchor (e.g., breath) and gently and nonjudgmentally reorienting attention back. This strengthens the attentional muscle.

Explain the benefits of combining mindfulness with activities like walking meditation, where you pair each step with conscious breathing. Being in nature engages multiple senses to maintain focus.

Suggest using grounding techniques like noticing five things you see, four things you hear, three things you feel, two things you smell, and one thing you taste as a quick way to stay present when thoughts become distracting.

Mindful listening exercises, such as focusing intently on a podcast or audiobook doing nothing else, help with listening comprehension and attention span.

Mindful technologies can support regular practice, such as meditation apps with nature sounds or a mindfulness bell set at intervals to remind you to pause and check your state of mind.

Encourage keeping a daily mindfulness journal to log favourite practices and any insights, feelings or ways you notice improvements in focus, stress or well-being. This nurtures self-awareness.

Highlight the community-building benefits of joining an in-person or online meditation group, such as staying motivated and learning different techniques through sharing experiences.

The aim would be to provide various mindfulness tools and tips that readers can experiment with to develop an attention training routine tailored to their specific needs and lifestyle. Consistency is critical for neuroplastic benefit.

Brain Training Games and Computer Programs

Brain training computer programs and mobile apps are designed to scientifically challenge different cognitive functions through stimulating games and puzzles. Popular options like Lumosity, Elevate, and Happy Neuron include exercises targeting working memory, problem-solving, attention, and visual processing skills. The games work by progressively increasing in difficulty as your abilities improve. They are personalised to provide customised "workouts" tailored to your needs. Most programs incorporate assessments to track your performance over time and monitor progress. If practised consistently, using 10-15 minutes daily has been clinically shown to help enhance focus, memory, planning, and overall mental agility. The games provide a fun, engaging way to supplement other focus techniques by regularly "exercising" your brain. Looking for programs incorporated into research studies can help validate their effectiveness. Varying the games between sessions targets a wide range of cognition. Brain training breaks when mentally fatigued can reinvigorate your focus and apply it to studies or work.

In more detail, popular programs provide customised routines of puzzles, mental challenges, visual and auditory tests, maths problems, and more. Your performance creates an individually calibrated regimen that stimulates specific cognitive functions identified as areas for improvement. Progressively more challenging levels push your brain to form new connections—integrated assessments chart skills development, such as reasoning, over weeks/months of regular use. The gameplay is designed not to feel like a chore, so it stays motivating to build cognition through enjoyable challenges. Programs are played in short sessions incorporated as a supplemental habit alongside other focus techniques for best results.

Brain training games strengthen cognitive abilities through adaptive mental challenges that target specific functions like working memory, problem-solving, and attention. As neuroimaging studies show, regular practice stimulates neuroplasticity, forming new neural connections and increasing volumes of associated brain regions. Improvements generalise to untrained skills since foundational processes are enhanced, not just activities. Popular options provide personalised routines and integrated assessments to track customised development. Daily 10–15 minute sessions deliver fun, engaging exercises that develop focus, memory, and agility when practised constantly for weeks or months. Varying the gameplay between a wide range of stimulating puzzles and activities best challenges the brain while balancing physical and sedentary trainers maximises cross-domain benefits. Individualising program elements based on baseline profiles, lifestyle, and preferences optimise impact. These evidence-based strategies reinforce attention pathways through enjoyable mental workouts that transfer to applicable skills like learning.

Critical Benefits of Brain Training Games And Programs

Brain training games have many cognitive and mental health benefits when practised regularly. Consistent training strengthens neural connections in the brain and can even increase grey matter in regions associated with the skills being targeted. This enhances functions like memory, attention, problem-solving, and mental processing speed over both the short and long term. Just 10-15 minutes per day of personalised challenges have been shown to improve cognitive reserve, making the brain more equipped to combat age-related decline.

Beyond shielding against future issues, brain training also provides immediate benefits to focus, concentration, and learning abilities that can boost productivity and mood. The stimulating, engaging nature of digital games fosters motivation to adhere to routines compared to rote mental drills. Their personalised nature and flexibility allow for custom workouts on any schedule. Short sessions have cumulative benefits beyond occasional long sessions, keeping the ageing brain active and engaged. Brain training is a fun, effective way to supplement other focus methods and potentially gain protection for cognitive health long into the future.

Key benefits of brain training games and programs:

Explain how brain training improves cognitive reserve by stimulating neuroplasticity and fostering new neural connections. Complex, variable challenges promote beneficial changes to brain structure and function.

Cite specific studies that used MRI/fMRI to show brain training is associated with increased grey matter volume and blood flow to targeted neural regions involved in processing speed, memory, problem-solving, etc.

Note that brain training improves performance on the trained tasks and often transfers to gains in untrained cognitive abilities due to enhanced underlying executive functions/mental processes. This far-transfer effect is essential.

Discuss how brain training reduces fatigue, stress, and anxiety symptoms by requiring focused engagement to complete tasks. The relaxed state induced helps mental recovery and optimisation.

Brain training games are self-paced and provide ongoing performance feedback as natural rewards, motivating continued participation to witness progress.

Highlight newer programs combining brain training with physical activity/social elements to leverage cross-domain benefits on cognition, mood, and longevity from a multi-dimensional approach.

Suggested variety is vital for maximum benefits (e.g. switching up game types, levels, and cognitive domains targeted) to continually challenge the brain in new ways.

Popular Brain Training Programs:

Lumosity

It offers a wide range of game types that target different cognitive functions. The free version provides limited access, while premium subscriptions allow customised routines and progress tracking. Exercise topics include attention, memory, problem-solving, and spatial orientation. It has a large user base, and ongoing research supports its effectiveness. Lumosity is one of the most popular brain training programs, with a wide selection of game types scientifically developed to target discrete cognitive functions. Based on over 70 published studies, exercises are carefully designed to adapt to difficulty as individual performance improves continuously. Long-term research has linked practising Lumosity's memory, problem-solving, attention and flexibility games for 15-30 minutes per week to meaningful improvements in focus, processing speed and recall abilities within six weeks. Premium memberships incorporate comprehensive baseline assessments to provide personalised routines tailored to cognitive goals. Integrated mobile apps allow accessible training anywhere to synergise with any lifestyle. Extensive research-backed iterations aim to optimise the program by continually analysing aggregate gameplay data from a large user base. Many university and independent clinical trials provide real-world evidence supporting cognitive and quality-of-life benefits for older adults and clinical populations when using Lumosity long-term as part of a healthy brain lifestyle.

Elevate

Elevate provides personalised cognitive training programs through an initial thorough baseline assessment to identify individual strengths and weaknesses. Neuroscientists designed the program with input from academic researchers to optimise brain fitness outcomes. Users then follow 4–12-week training cycles with challenging daily exercises focused on targeted improvement areas, such as visual processing speed, cognitive flexibility, and working memory. Progress is carefully tracked throughout training. Elevate features over 50 unique board game-style activities that continually adapt to the difficulty level based on individual performance to challenge the brain continuously. Training incorporates the latest neuroscience on neuroplasticity and cognitive load principles to stimulate cognitive abilities effectively. Research has shown that training with Elevate can significantly boost processing speed, memory, attention, and executive function in just

12 weeks when completed in 5-10 minutes per day. Its rigorous scientific foundation and customised approach make Elevate an effective brain training option for cognitive enhancement.

Users complete brief tests to establish personalised baseline cognitive abilities. The program then prescribes challenging exercises focused on improvement areas. Progress is monitored over 4–12-week training cycles. Exercises stimulate visual processing speed, cognitive flexibility, and working memory. It incorporates the science of neuroplasticity and cognitive load.

Happy Neuron

Happy Neuron takes a whole-brain approach to cognitive stimulation through a collection of over 25 colourful and accessible brain games. Puzzles are designed to gently challenge functions across different cognitive domains, including logic, maths skills, visual perception, and language comprehension, at an individual's own pace. Each week, a new challenge is unlocked to maintain long-term engagement through varied gameplay. The games use learning theory best practices to reinforce connections through feedback and increasing difficulty levels based on performance over time. While it does not provide the same specialised personalised training routines as programs like Lumosity or Elevate, research shows regular casual gameplay can still help boost overall brain health and protect cognitive functioning in ageing adults. Even moderate use of 10-15 minutes a few times a week has improved mental clarity and focus by stimulating broad cognitive processes when paired with other brain-healthy habits like social activity and exercise.

It features over 25 colourful brain game options for all levels. Puzzles work on functions like logic, math skills, visual perception, and language comprehension. A new challenge is unlocked each week to keep it engaging. It takes a whole-brain approach and incorporates learning theory best practices. It provides general cognitive stimulation rather than specialised training routines.

Peak

Peak provides the most comprehensive cognitive assessments of any brain training program, analysing up to 14 mental skills through in-depth pre- and post-training evaluations. This allows for highly personalised workout prescriptions targeting identified individual cognitive weaknesses. Users then follow adaptive schedules of personalised daily exercises delivered across web and mobile platforms. Peak's workouts are carefully tailored based on baseline profiles and continually adjust in difficulty level to challenge trainees' improving abilities. Extensive clinical research validates Peak's effectiveness, showing significant gains in abilities like self-control, memory, processing speed and fluid intelligence after consistent use of just 10-15 minutes per day for 8-12 weeks. No other brain fitness program has more academic validation studies confirming real-world cognitive benefits. This rigorous scientific foundation has made Peak a trusted solution that is widely used in clinical settings and adopted in school curriculums to help enhance students' mental performance.

Offers in-depth pre- and post-cognitive assessments analysing 14 mental abilities. A detailed personalised training profile targeting specific weaknesses is created based on baseline results. Workouts are prescribed across the web and mobile in adaptive schedules. It has extensive research validating improvements and is widely used clinically and in schools.

Mind Research Institute

The Mind Research Institute takes a specialised approach to cognitive training through games that build spatial-temporal reasoning and numerical intuition from a young age. Exercises unfold conceptual STEM skills by engaging different visual-spatial abilities. Research has found that it is used extensively in after-school programs to enhance problem-solving strategies for maths challenges. By developing natural number sense, Mind Research Institute aims to cultivate interests and aptitudes for students who may later pursue STEM degrees and careers. Its curriculum has shown potential for helping with more advanced abstract mathematical thinking from an early educational stage when the brain is most malleable. Combining specialised cognitive tools with broader lifestyle transformations covered in this chapter empowers lifelong learners of all ages to strengthen discrete thinking areas and global mental fitness through evidence-backed, multi-modal techniques selected appropriately for individuals' needs and interests.

Focuses specifically on building maths intuitive thinking through spatial-temporal reasoning exercises. Games involve unfolding numerical and geometric concepts. Used extensively in after-school programs, it aims to develop STEM skills from a young age.

In this chapter, we covered many evidence-based techniques and tools that can be utilised to strengthen focus and cognitive abilities. We learned about establishing good routines through mindfulness, proper sleep, exercise, and nutrition habits. We explored concepts like neuroplasticity, showing how the brain remains modifiable throughout life. We discussed Pomodoro-style time blocking and limiting distractions to maximise productivity during dedicated focus periods. Brain training games were highlighted as a supplemental method to regularly challenge the mind through stimulating exercises. Understanding mindfulness skills like breathwork and body scans provides calming strategies to reduce stress and boost concentration. Implementing different cognitive strategies situationally and combining habits over the long term empowers us to take control of our mental performance and set ourselves up for success in school, work, and beyond through optimised focus and thinking skills.

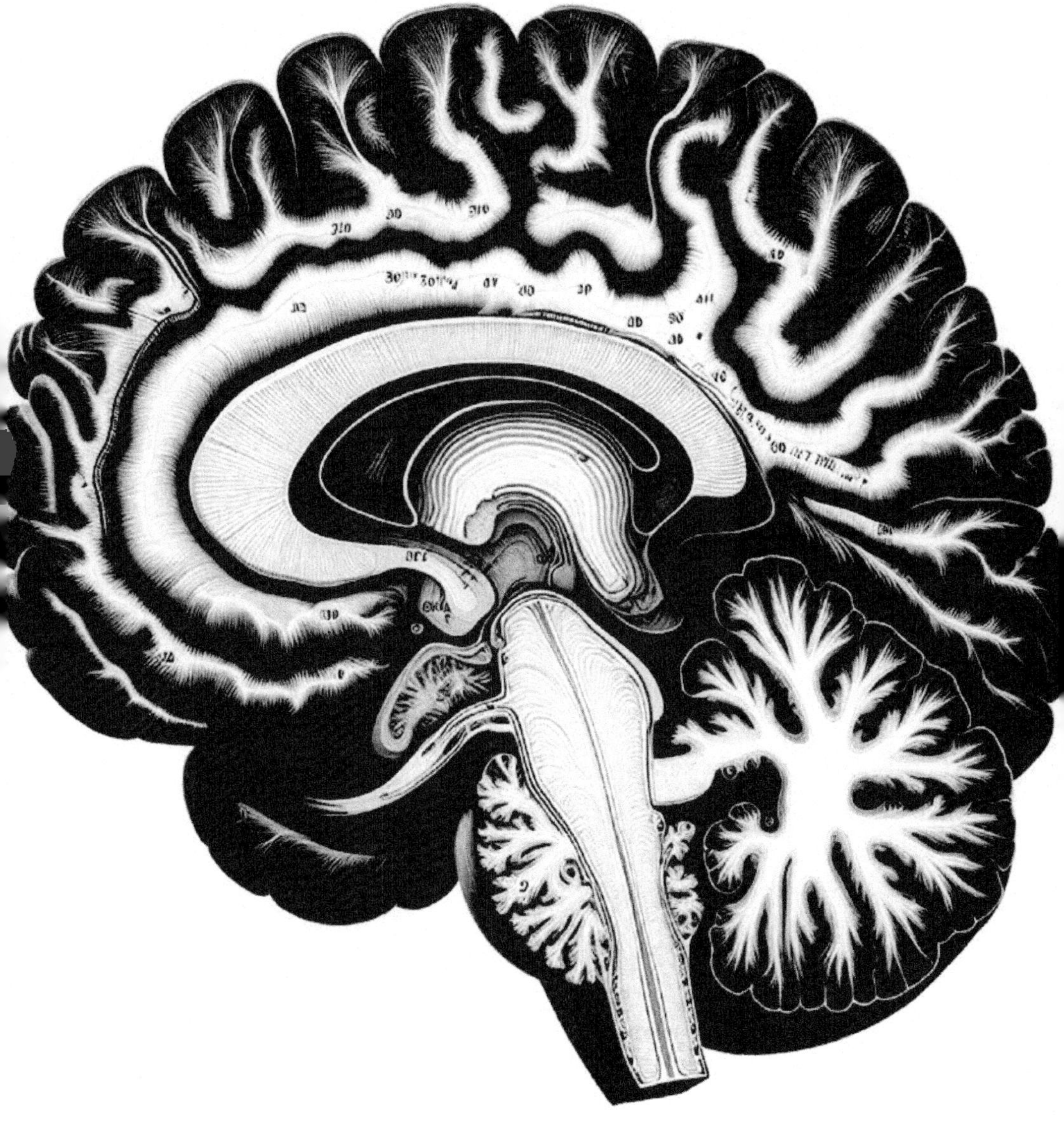

Survivor's Note

Remember that Rome wasn't built in a day.

Developing laser-like concentration takes patience and practice. Start small if you need to, just five focused minutes at first. Celebrate the little wins.

On challenging days, remember why developing focus matters to you. How will sharpening your mental abilities serve your goals and dreams?

Remembering the bigger picture can inspire you to keep going. You've got this. When you notice your attention drifting, lovingly guide it back. Over time, those neural pathways will develop into highways of hyper-focus. Discover which strategies work best for you - music, timers, or standing desks.

Each moment you choose presence over distractions brings you closer to your best self. I have complete faith in your ability to transform.

You were born for this. Now show your amazing brain who's boss! I'm cheering you on.

FRONTAL LOBE   PARIENTAL LOBE

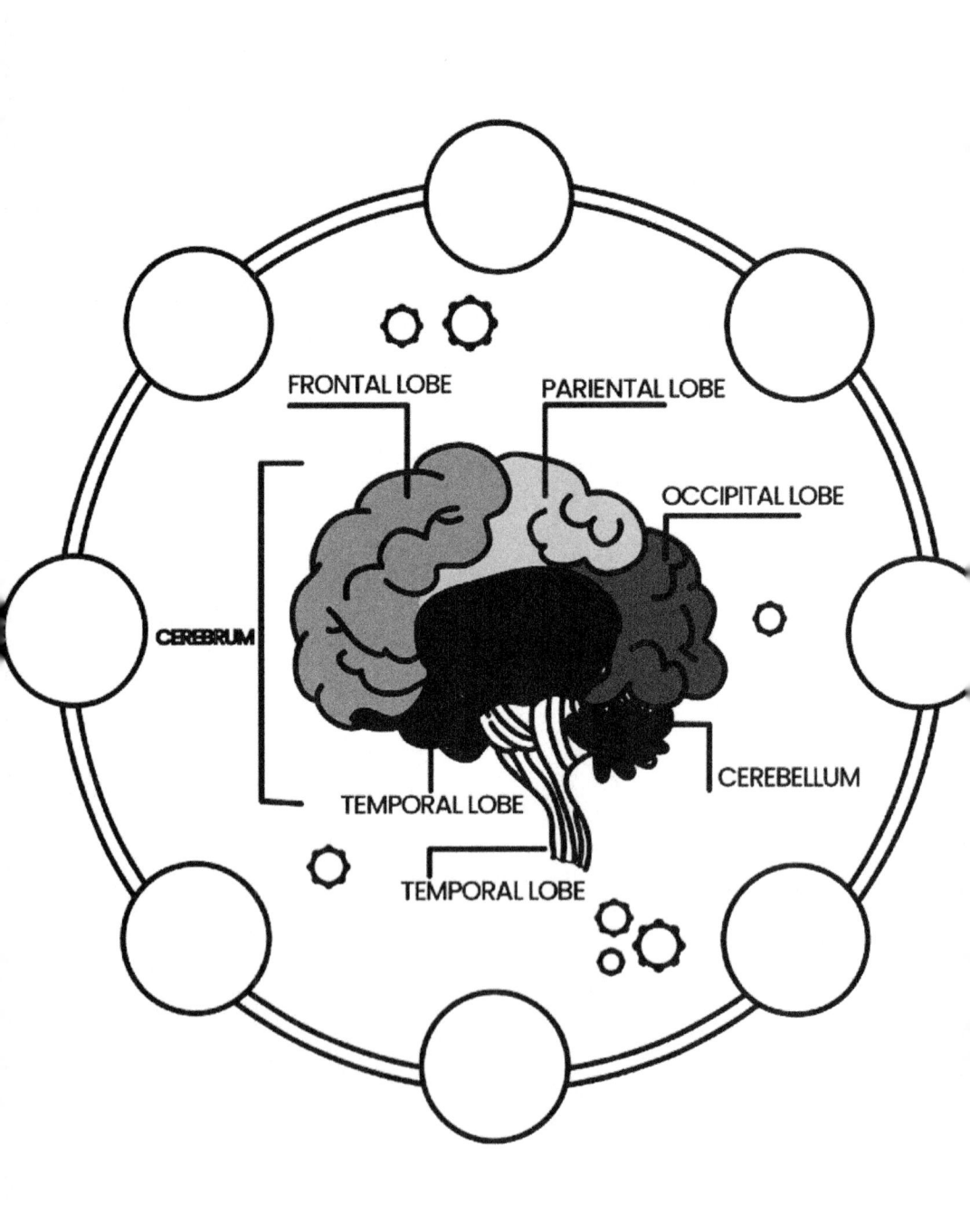

OCCIPITAL LOBE

CEREBRUM

CEREBELLUM

TEMPORAL LOBE

TEMPORAL LOBE

CHAPTER 4

Improving Working Memory

Neuroimaging research has provided insights into the brain differences underlying working memory challenges in ADHD. Studies utilising fMRI and other techniques have found that individuals with ADHD show less activity in the prefrontal cortex region of the brain during working memory tasks compared to those without ADHD. The prefrontal cortex plays a critical role in executive functions such as attention regulation, planning, problem-solving, and short-term memory.

Deficits in both verbal and visual-spatial working memory domains have been consistently seen through meta-analyses and individual experimental studies. Tasks requiring participants to temporarily hold information in mind and mentally manipulate it, such as recalling letters in reverse order or replacing letters with new ones, show reduced performance among ADHD groups. One commonly used measure is the n-back test, where individuals must identify if the current stimulus matches the one in trials previously. Those with ADHD usually have lower accuracy and slower response times on these tests, especially as the load level increases.

Research suggests working memory impairments may represent a core underlying deficit in ADHD. The compromised ability to temporarily maintain goal information and task details online could negatively affect other executive functions that rely on working memory resources. Studies also indicate these working memory challenges persist throughout development, from childhood through adulthood, rather than being outgrown. Robust evidence shows working memory as a valid cognitive marker and lifelong impairment associated with the diagnosis of ADHD.

Here are some visualisation and repetition strategies that can help improve working memory for those with ADHD:

Visualisation Strategies

Visualisation is a powerful cognitive tool that activates more of the brain than verbal processing alone. When new information is encoded linguistically and spatially through vivid mental imagery, it becomes more readily retrievable. Several techniques tap into this dual-coding advantage:

Create mental images to associate new information with familiar concepts. For example, visualise each item on a shopping list as an object in a memorable scene.

Use visualisation techniques like mind maps and diagrams or draw out key points to capture information spatially in the mind.

Imagine walking through your house, school, etc., and placing information you need to recall in different rooms or locations.

Repetition Strategies

Repetition is one of the most powerful, scientifically validated techniques for optimising memory formation and recall. When information is re-exposed to the brain repeatedly over spaced intervals, it gets cemented into long-term stores more enduringly. A few evidence-based methods leverage repetition:

Repeat information aloud or by writing it down several times to reinforce memory encoding. Playback recordings as a review.

Quiz yourself on content regularly with flashcards, games, or drilling with a study partner for continuous practice.

Break down large chunks of information into smaller, repeated study sessions over time rather than long cramming.

Use mnemonic devices like acronyms, songs, or rhymes to make the repetitive recall of various facts more engaging.

Connect new ideas to previously learned concepts whenever possible, embedding them into existing cognitive schemas through repeated exposure.

Active visualisation and frequent repetition of information are effective techniques supported by research to help strengthen working memory function impaired by ADHD. One strategy involves creating vivid mental images that associate new concepts to be learned with familiar visual representations stored in long-term memory. Imagining each item on a grocery list as an object in a memorable scene, for example, engages spatial reasoning areas of the brain to encode the information more deeply. Drawing diagrams, graphs, or other visual depictions of key ideas captures them spatially through the mind's eye. Imagining placing details mentally at different locations within a familiar environment, like rooms in a house, provides similar benefits. Repeated rehearsal through verbal repetition, writing notes multiple times, turning facts into catchy songs or rhymes, or quizzing oneself regularly with flashcards or games directs focus to the target material often for continual reinforcement of fragile working memory traces at risk for fading. Over time, embedding new ideas into schema through integrating them with prior knowledge as a framework aids long-term retention. Such multisensory, hands-on approaches are useful for many with ADHD by evading weak unimodal memory systems in favour of better-supported neurological pathways.

These active, multisensory methods aim to strengthen weak working memory through visualisation pathways in the brain and habituating information through frequent retrieval practice and review.

The memory palace technique capitalises on the brain's robust ability to remember spatial information by using vivid imagery placed in familiar locations. Cognitive research has shown the effectiveness of this method, known as the

Method of Loci, for improving recall. In one study, researchers found participants could remember up to 80% of words encoded using a memory palace compared to only 20% without the technique. It involves developing a clear mental picture of an environment memorised in its details, like one's childhood home or current residence. Various pieces of information to be recalled are then assigned visual representations and strategically "placed" in different spots throughout the imagined location using as many senses as possible.

Another effective visual-spatial strategy is creating mind maps to organise related concepts. Neuroimaging research shows that mind mapping activates the same brain regions involved in spatial navigation. These diagrams begin with a central topic and branch out major ideas connected by lines with key details along them. Repeatedly reviewing the mind map strengthens fragile working memory traces through continual reinforcement. Both techniques bypass typical unimodal weaknesses for those with ADHD by encoding information multimodally into strong long-term memory domains, as shown by improved recall on memory tests.

The memory palace technique and mind maps for improving working memory:

Memory Palace Technique

The Memory Palace technique, also known as the Method of Loci, is an effective visualisation strategy that taps into the mental mapping ability of spatial memory:

Also called a "memory journey," the Memory Palace uses the associative encoding advantages of vivid spatial imagery. By mentally placing items to be remembered in specific locations along a familiar route or setting, abstract concepts are linked to concrete places already well-established in long-term memory.

Develop a vivid mental image of a well-known location, like your house or childhood home.

Assign pieces of information to different rooms, furnishings, or spots along a familiar route.

"Place" each item visually in the assigned place through imagination. For example, put your grocery list on the kitchen table.

You can mentally recall all the items by "walking through" your memory palace. The more senses are used, the stronger the memory trace.

Mind Maps:

Mind maps are a Potent note-taking and revision technique that utilises the strengths of visual-spatial thinking:

Author Tony Buzan popularised the mind map as a dynamic diagramming style that mirrors how the brain naturally encodes information in associative networks.

Mind maps activate more brain regions than linear notes by incorporating mental paths and visual representations. Some key aspects include:

Start with a central concept or topic in the middle of a blank page.

Draw branches extending out and connecting to associated ideas, with keywords placed along the lines.

Use images, colours, and visual organisation to represent connections between related concepts in a radiating structure.

Mind maps activate more of the brain than plain text by incorporating visual spatial abilities.

Tracing the logical flow repeatedly aids retention, and adding details over time is easy.

Both techniques use strong visual memory capabilities to supplement weak working memory limitations. Unlike regular studies, imaginative, multisensory approaches effectively embed information through neurological pathways.

External Aids

External aids are practical tools that can strengthen focus and compensate for weaknesses in natural working memory capacity:

Our biological working memory is limited, so offloading responsibilities and details onto physical reminders lightens the cognitive load. Checklists, calendar notifications, labels, and other external memory cues let critical information remain accessible despite an individual's attention level. A few methods include:

External aids Like reminders and checklists can help improve working memory for tasks:

Checklists keep information explicit rather than relying on memory alone. Physical reminders of steps and responsibilities prevent critical details from falling through the cracks.

Apps, calendars, and notifications on phones and computers prompt users for upcoming tasks, appointments, or deadlines. Time-based reminders compensate for a poor internal sense of time.

Sticky notes or whiteboards in visible locations display important to-dos, numbers to call, formulas to remember, etc. Physical reminder cues in the environment aid retrieval.

Organisation systems like colour-coded binders and labelled folders for paperwork optimise finding important documents later. They also reduce the stress of losing or misfiling critical records.

Labels, photos, or diagrams on storage containers help recall where items are stored to avoid wasted time searching. Visual prompts serve as external memory.

Reading checklists or notes out loud or having someone else review them reinforces encoding through an additional modality like speech.

Relying on external memory aids takes advantage of environmental triggers to prompt recall. This compensates for fragile working memory and reduces cognitive load, freeing resources for learning and complex thought.

Checklists, calendars, reminders, and other prompts provide essential scaffolding for individuals with ADHD to offload some memory responsibilities externally. Recording details of tasks, assignments, appointments, and deadlines reduces the cognitive load of remembering everything independently. Time-based alerts on phones and computers help those struggling with time blindness.

Well-organised systems for paperwork, notes, and other materials minimise wasted mental effort when searching or backtracking. Colour-coding, labelling, and photos directly on storage containers serve as a type of "external brain" that improves easy access to information without taxing fragile working memory. Embedding critical materials like checklists and reference guides where needed enhances on-the-spot usability rather than relying on recalling to retrieve them later.

Using visual and verbal modalities to learn and review checklists, instructions, and other materials strengthens memory encoding through multiple pathways. It offers backup retrieval routes if one is forgotten. External frameworks promote logically carrying out multi-step activities sequentially according to existing knowledge structures. This reduces errors from lapses in attention, organisation, or memory compared to unstructured attempts without this support.

Over time, reliable use of memory aids can help automate routines and processes through learned procedural memory. This places fewer unpredictable demands on fallible executive functions controlling consciously-driven cognition and behaviour. The goal is to optimise higher-order thinking by outsourcing avoidable memory burdens to reliable environmental prompts and systems.

This chapter discussed various evidence-based techniques for strengthening working memory challenges associated with ADHD. It began by exploring findings from neuroimaging and cognitive studies demonstrating the robust nature of visual spatial memory pathways compared to weakened verbal working memory, typically impaired in ADHD.

Effective visualisation strategies were presented, such as the Memory Palace method and mind maps. These strategies take advantage of long-term solid spatial representation abilities. Repetition through flashcards, note-taking, and self-testing were also reviewed as beneficial for continuously reinforcing new information through retrieval practice.

Using external aids like checklists, reminders, organisational systems, and direct physical cues in the environment was covered in depth. By offloading memory responsibilities externally, such strategies compensate for fragile, temporary memory traces prone to fading. Multimodal encoding through visual and verbal channels was explained to bolster memory encoding and retrieval.

Over time, it was noted these techniques can help automate routines to place fewer unpredictable demands on self-regulation abilities. The goal of optimising higher-order cognitive skills by outsourcing avoidable memory processes to reliable environmental supports formed an essential conclusion. The chapter summarised research-backed memory strategies for improving learning and task completion challenges faced by many with ADHD.

ADHD Research Findings

A review of structural neuroimaging studies of ADHD (Faraone et al., 2015) found consistent evidence of reduced grey matter volume and thickness in regions of the prefrontal cortex and cerebellum in children and adults with ADHD relative to controls. A meta-analysis of 40 functional MRI studies (Cortese et al., 2012) also found hypoactivity in frontostriatal and fronto-cerebellar circuits related to attention, inhibition and executive function in individuals with ADHD.

Multiple genome-wide association studies have identified several genes associated with an increased risk of ADHD, including genes involved in dopamine and norepinephrine signalling pathways (Franke et al., 2012; Hamshere et al., 2013). A meta-analysis by Gizer et al. (2009) confirmed the role of several candidate genes in ADHD risk.

A longitudinal twin study by Cherkasova et al. (2013) found heritability estimates of ADHD symptoms ranging from 70-80%, highlighting the important genetic component. Environmental factors such as low birth weight, perinatal stress, childhood trauma, and socioeconomic status have also been correlated with ADHD outcomes in epidemiological research (Banerjee et al., 2007; Langley et al., 2010).

Neuropsychological research consistently shows deficits in core executive functions of working memory, inhibition, time management and planning in individuals with ADHD (Willcutt et al., 2005; Metzler-Baddeley & Jones, 2017). Co-morbidity is also highly prevalent, with about 65% of children with ADHD having at least one additional psychiatric diagnosis (Larson et al., 2011).

Research utilising multiple methodologies has provided compelling evidence that ADHD is a neurodevelopmental disorder associated with genetic and environmental risk factors and neurobiological deficits in frontostriatal brain circuits.

FRONTAL LOBE   PARIENTAL LOBE

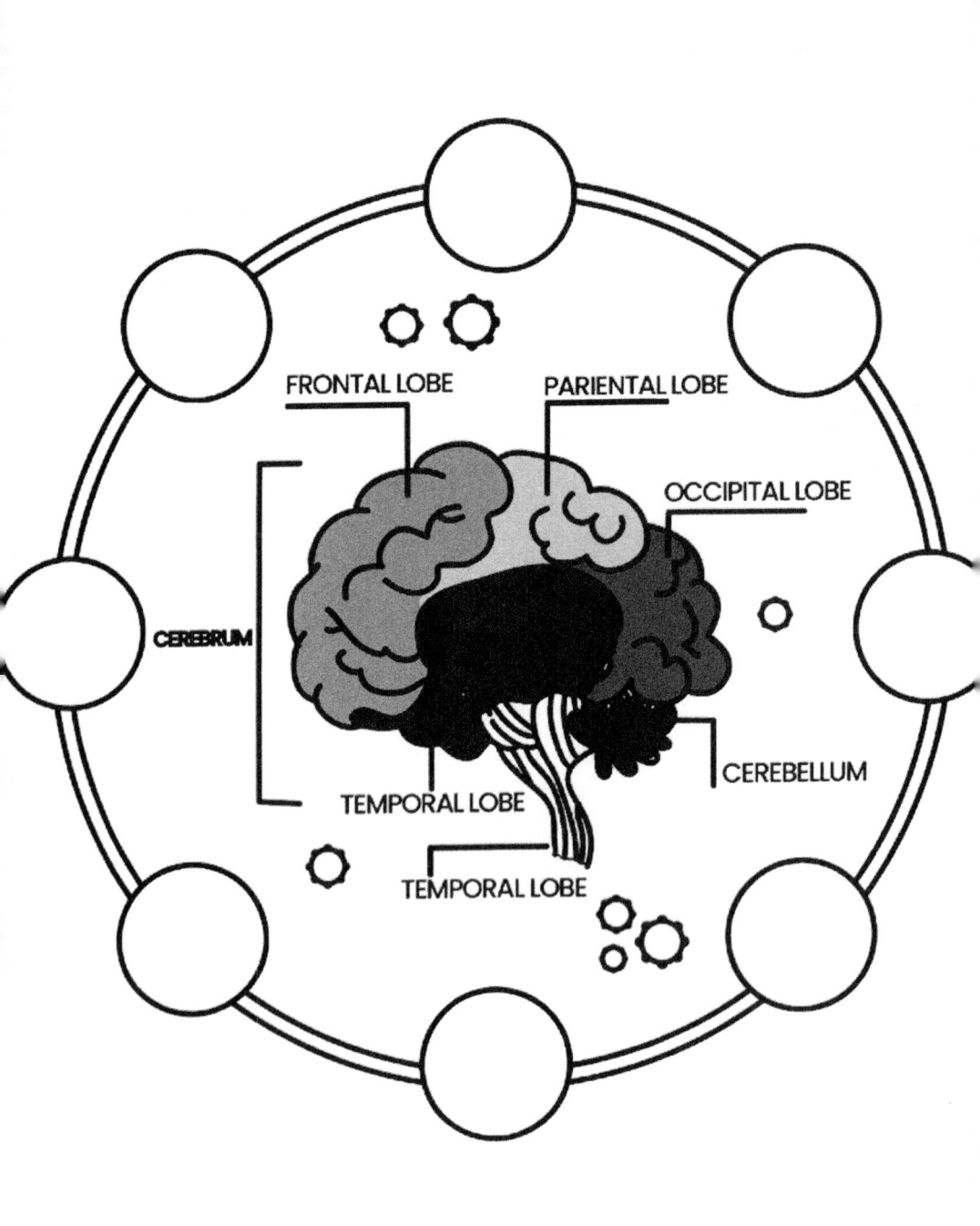

OCCIPITAL LOBE

CEREBRUM

CEREBELLUM

TEMPORAL LOBE

TEMPORAL LOBE

CHAPTER 5

Enhancing Time Management

Time blindness is a hallmark challenge for many people living with ADHD. It refers to impairments in perceiving the subjective experience of time passing and difficulties in accurately estimating durations. For those with ADHD, weaknesses in prefrontal cortical regions involved in temporal processing cause abnormalities in internally gauging the pace of ongoing events and keeping a clear sense of chronology. Hours may feel like minutes or drawn out gradually, distorting the perception of time's continuity. This time blindness makes it hard to judge how long tasks will take to complete or stay on a consistent schedule. Deadlines lose their urgency due to a lack of intuitive awareness of time remaining. The consequence is often last-minute scrambling, tardiness, poor planning, and failure to finish assignments within expected durations.

External supports like calendars, alarms, timers, and breaking work into small intervals can help provide a structure that bypasses weaknesses internally, tracking the passage of moments, minutes, and hours taken for granted by most.

Time management is one of the biggest challenges faced by individuals with ADHD due to issues with time blindness and difficulty estimating the passage of time. If left unaddressed, problems with poor time awareness can seriously affect work efficiency, academic or career success, and fulfilling responsibilities on schedule. In this article, we will explore evidence-based strategies for externally imposing structure on time to compensate for weaknesses in internally perceiving duration and planning time use. Specifically, we will cover the techniques of calendar blocking and using scheduling templates to map out time commitments on a calendar or planner in an organised, visual manner. These approaches help condition a routine sense of time, bypassing impairments in perceiving moments and hours' subjective flow.

Calendar blocking involves scheduling each time commitment and period of focused work on a calendar in dedicated blocks of time.

It provides an external visual structure to time to compensate for difficulties internally tracking the passage of hours.

A pre-scheduled calendar holds the individual accountable for starting and stopping tasks as scheduled.

Templates can help with calendar blocking by providing ready-made daily/weekly schedules to fill in tasks and commitments.

Examples include templates that schedule work/leisure hours, separate blocks for personal vs. professional tasks, or protecting morning/afternoon slots for deep work.

Scheduling templates condition time blindness by providing routine, predictable timeframes that feel less ambiguous.

They discourage slack time and can seem invisible to those with weak internal time awareness.

Scheduling back-to-back blocks keeps momentum vs breaks, leading to off-task behaviour.

Templates also help to envision how tasks will fit in upcoming weeks/days for better planning.

In addition to implementing calendar blocking and scheduling templates, various alert systems, timers, and organisers can strengthen routine time management for those with time blindness. Externally imposing structure on time use helps compensate for weaknesses in internally perceiving duration and temporal planning. This next section will explore more strategies centred around digital and written reminders that provide recurrent time cues and accountability checks. Specifically, we will cover how setting timers, alarms, and recurring calendar alerts and using daily planners and to-do lists can lend routine timing support that bypasses impairments experiencing the subjective passage of moments.

Setting timers and alarm prompts to start and stop tasks per a scheduled calendar. This external cue transitions versus relying on poor internal time sense.

Timers on electronic devices or standalone timers limit distractions by letting users focus on one activity at a time for short, defined periods.

Recurring alerts remind us of future tasks, appointments, and deadlines to combat weak future time perspectives. Push notifications on calendars help with last-minute scheduling.

Organisers like daily/weekly planners, to-do lists, and task apps provide a single written record of commitments. Checking off completed items boosts accountability and feelings of productivity.

Colour-coded organisers (e.g., red for urgent tasks) visually denote priorities to lend structure absent from internal time perceptions.

Travel organisers help stay on schedule when away from a regular environment without routine time cues.

Breaking activities into incremental steps tracked on organisers or spreadsheets prevents underestimating the demands of large blocks of open-ended time.

Reviewing organisers aloud verbally reinforces encoding commitments through an additional modality to aid recall.

Accountability partners provide important external motivation and oversight for those with time blindness due to ADHD. Studies show people are more likely to follow through on commitments when they know someone will check their progress (Hall et al., 2014). An accountability partner can help overcome weak intrinsic prioritisation by agreeing to check in during scheduled windows to discuss barriers and problem-solve solutions (Philip et al., 2022). They also boost accuracy by reviewing calendars together and asking questions about upcoming events, leveraging the memory of another to compensate for impaired time perception (Pirbaglou et al., 2013). Simply communicating commitments to an accountability partner makes the intentions more concrete and tangible, improving the chances of following through (Wood & Rünger, 2016).

Accountability partners provide a backup form of time awareness when an individual's internal perception feels uncertain. They foster self-awareness around weaknesses by offering honest feedback (Zargar et al., 2022). This encourages compensation through structured habits and routines over the long term as skills develop. Research finds that enlisting social support is critical to successfully implementing executive function strategies for ADHD in natural settings over months (Sibley et al., 2018). Accountability relationships thus cultivate routines by conditioning behaviour externally to bypass time blindness.

We have discussed several evidence-based approaches for improving time management challenges associated with weakness in perceiving the passage of time, known as time blindness. Calendar blocking and scheduling templates provide important external structure by mapping out time commitments and periods for focused work in advance. Setting recurring alert timers and using organisers impart additional routine timing cues. Together, these strategies compensate for impairments in internal sensing duration by imposing predictable routines.

Enlisting accountability partners further strengthens schedule implementation and commitment to deadlines. They lend social motivation and serve as a backup time awareness source through regular check-ins. These techniques aim to condition behaviours and scaffold new habits by bypassing weaknesses in intrinsic time perception. Gradual practice develops skills until compensation becomes more self-driven over time. The combination of planning, alerts, accountability, and routine builds stability from outside sources to address a core executive dysfunction for many with ADHD.

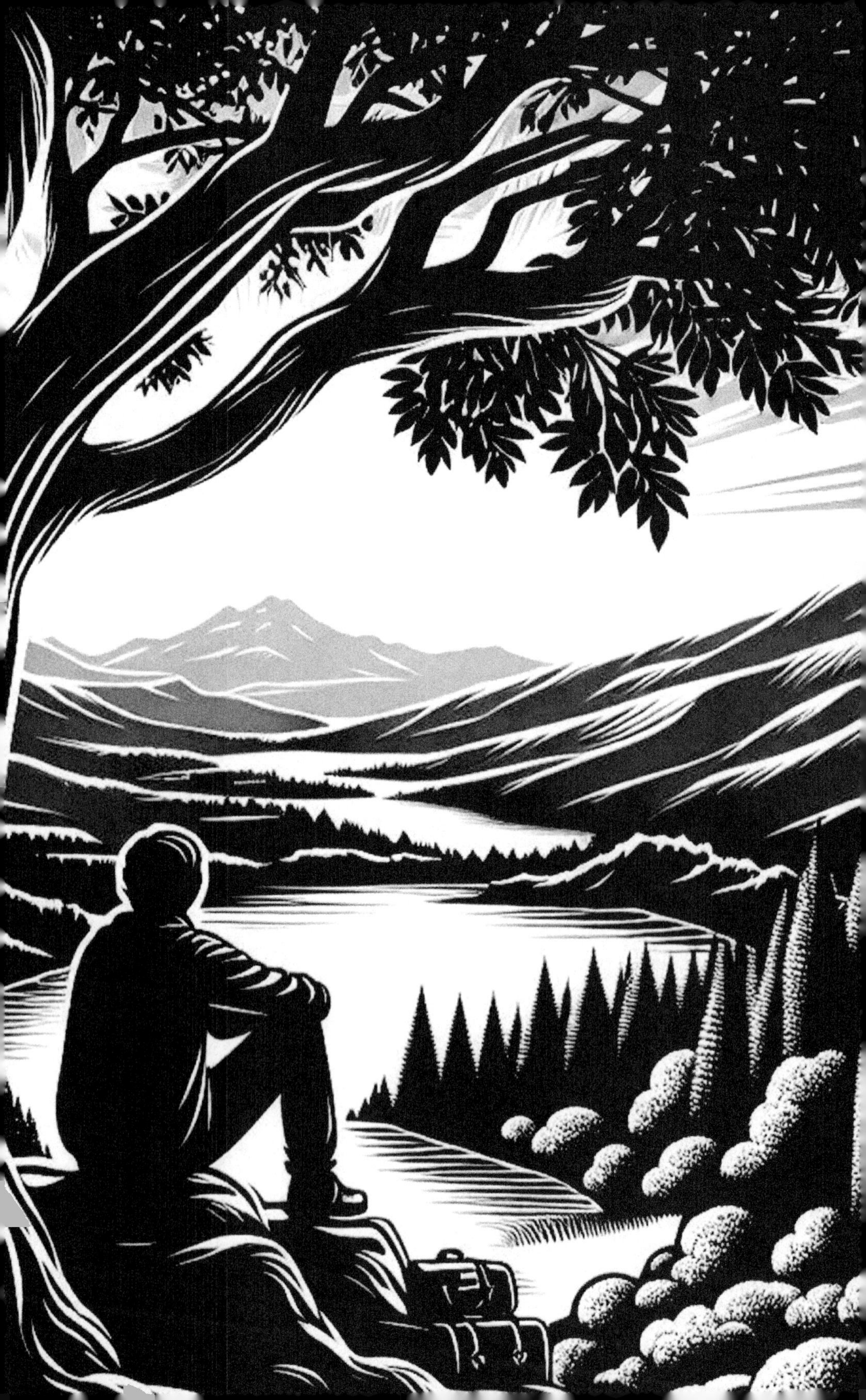

Survivor's Note

You've got this! I know managing time and staying on track can feel impossible some days with ADHD, but remember how far you've come already. Every strategy you've learned and habit you've formed is building your skills. Don't be too hard on yourself for mistakes - they're all part of the process. Just keep tweaking your system until you find what works.

You're allowing yourself to learn at your own pace.

When focusing feels futile, take a breather.

Come back to it refreshed later. Any one task doesn't define your worth.

FRONTAL LOBE   PARIENTAL LOBE

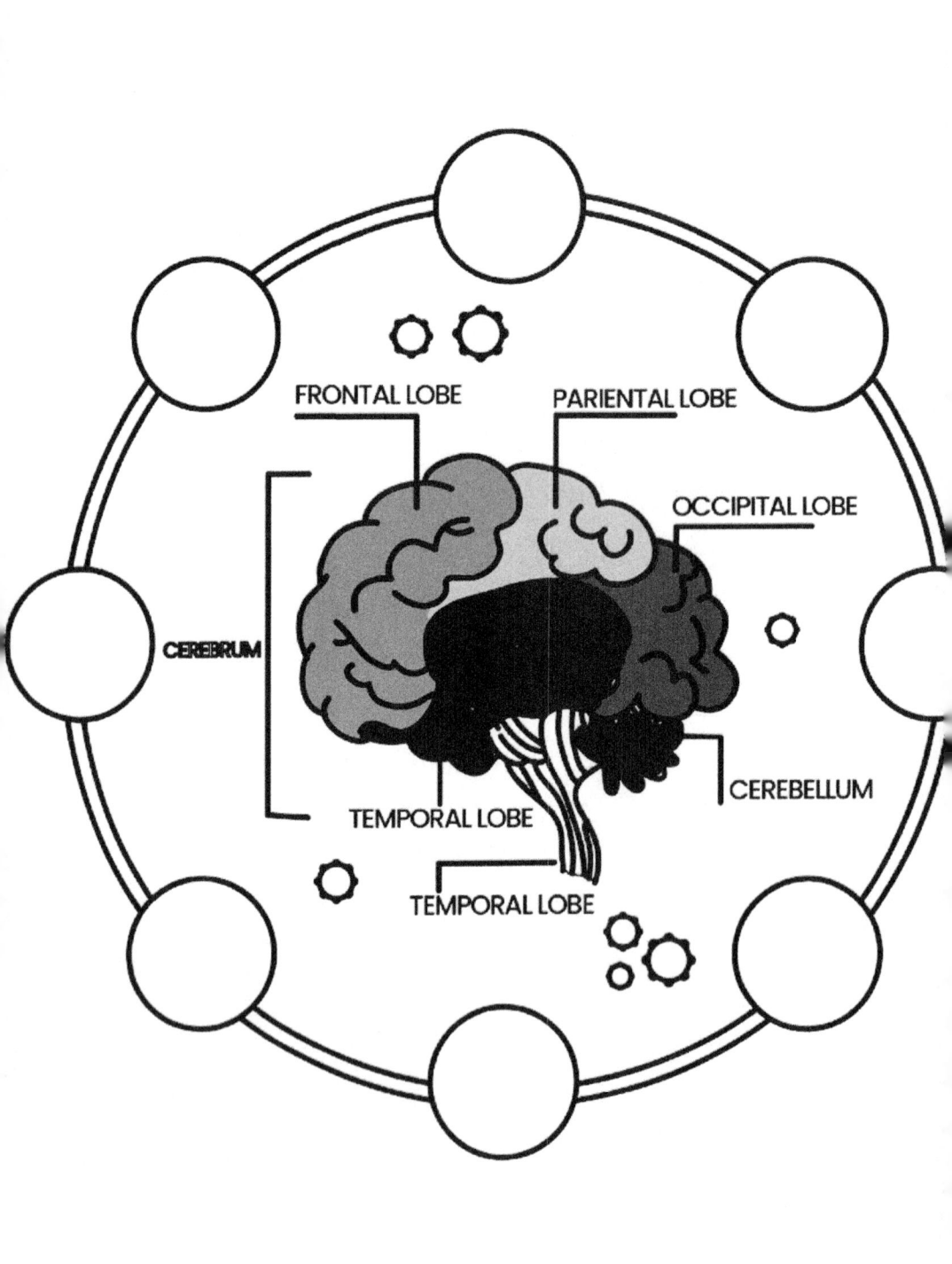

OCCIPITAL LOBE

CEREBRUM

CEREBELLUM

TEMPORAL LOBE

TEMPORAL LOBE

CHAPTER 6

Strengthening Motivation

For those with ADHD, maintaining motivation and following through on goals and tasks can be significant struggles due to impairments in executive functioning skills. Traditional goal-setting methods often fail because motivation is inconsistently intrinsic for ADHD brains. Research supports this, as a 2012 study published in the Journal of Abnormal Child Psychology found that children with ADHD relied more heavily on external rewards to stay motivated compared to their peers without ADHD. The dopamine dysfunction underpinning ADHD means motivation relies heavily on external structures and feedback systems. Left to instinctively self-motivate alone, focus is easily lost, and commitment breaks down. SMART goals directly address these challenges through built-in accountability and a sense of progress. By chunking projects into clear, discrete steps with deadlines, momentum remains high as frequent mini-successes satisfy the immediate dopamine needs inherent to ADHD. Measurable metrics also fulfil the need for quantifiable feedback on efforts. With motivation so closely tied to external motivation, structures like SMART goal setting are critical aids for ADHD survivors seeking to sustain energy on tasks over the long term. Strengthened motivation translates to improved self-determination, which benefits quality of life.

Rejection-sensitive dysphoria (RSD) is a common phenomenon experienced by about 30-50% of individuals with ADHD, according to research (Weyandt & DuPaul, 2008). RSD involves intense feelings of inadequacy, distress, or fear of rejection after only minor situations that could be perceived as negative feedback or criticism. This is thought to stem from having a rejection-specific hypersensitivity due to rejection experiences throughout childhood with undiagnosed ADHD (Drake et al., 2021). While RSD is debilitating at the moment, there are cognitive behavioral strategies shown to help mitigate its effect over the long term. Things like explaining RSD to close support systems, using daily self-affirmations to combat negative self-perceptions, cognitively challenging irrational rejections and fears through evidence, using mindfulness techniques to notice triggers without overreacting, pursuing confidence-building interests, and seeking counselling can support adaptive coping (Sibley et al., 2018). With the understanding and practice of such compensation strategies, the level of distress from RSD can be reduced.

Rejection-sensitive dysphoria (RSD) is a common issue faced by many individuals with Attention Deficit Hyperactivity Disorder (ADHD) that can significantly affect their well-being and relationships. RSD involves experiencing intense feelings of inadequacy, distress, or fear of rejection in response to even minor perceived criticisms or rejections. This heightened emotional sensitivity is thought to stem from a pattern of rejection experiences throughout childhood with undiagnosed ADHD. Left unaddressed, RSD can undermine self-esteem and hold those suffering from it back from pursuing opportunities or maintaining close relationships. However, with the right coping strategies used over time, the distress from RSD can be managed. Research has shown approaches to help alleviate RSD include healthily expressing emotions, practising self-care and positive self-talk, and cognitive restructuring.

Strategies for coping with rejection-sensitive dysphoria (RSD): healthily express your emotions, like writing in a journal, talking to a close friend, or exercising. Bottling up feelings can make RSD worse.

Permit yourself to say no without feeling guilty. Learn your limits to avoid burnout.

Practice positive self-talk. When negative thoughts arise, purposefully redirect them with encouraging mantras like "I'm capable" or "I've overcome challenges before."

Focus on intrinsic motivation rather than seeking constant external validation, which is difficult with RSD. Pursue activities you genuinely enjoy.

Notice when perfectionism stems from RSD fears, then allow yourself to be imperfect. Mistakes fuel growth, not failure.

Challenge all-or-nothing thinking patterns that fuel RSD, like "If I don't ace this, I'm a failure." Mistakes are part of learning.

Surround yourself with people who accept you for who you are rather than constantly seeking approval. Their unconditional support counters RSD.

Be patient with yourself as you work on managing RSD. Healing doesn't happen overnight. Celebrate every small victory.

For individuals with ADHD, developing effective systems of motivation and self-regulation can be pretty challenging due to weaknesses in executive functioning skills like impulse control and delayed gratification. Traditional reward models that only provide feedback intermittently or after long periods of work are often ineffective, as the immediate reinforcements needed by ADHD are not adequately met. However, research shows that structured reward systems focused on short-term goals and frequent positive feedback can help engage the interest and dopamine-seeking nature of ADHD beneficially. When rewards are tied closely to progress, provide enjoyment, and reaffirm successes along the process, motivation and sustaining of goals are enhanced. Some strategies to make reward systems more suitable for the ADHD experience include focusing on small wins through clear milestone-based rewards and intrinsic enjoyment.

Here are tips for implementing reward systems focused on small wins and enjoyment to help manage symptoms associated with ADHD:

Focus on progress, not perfection. Celebrate every small accomplishment to stay motivated through challenges.

Build in frequent mini-rewards for completing short-term goals instead of waiting long periods between rewards. This gratifies the immediate needs of ADHD.

Choose rewards linked to interests and known enjoyment to maximise payoff.

Tangible rewards may work better than abstract praise.

Settle a transparent points/rewards system with attainable thresholds to work towards. Tracking progress with points provides dopamine feedback.

Remember that intrinsic rewards, such as a sense of pride, flow states, or relief, can also motivate. Pick rewards meaningful to the individual.

Schedule rewards after goal achievements to strongly associate positive feelings with the behaviour.

Make rewards consistent, but allow occasional substitutes to keep it exciting long term. Rigidity risks demotivation.

Enlist accountability partners to suggest and confirm rewards, adding a social element of enjoyment and shared experience.

For individuals with ADHD, forming and maintaining productive habits can be tricky due to weaknesses in self-regulation and time management. Trackers that use mental contrasting help overcome these challenges. Mental contrasting involves envisioning the positive outcomes of achieving a goal while considering possible obstacles.

Trackers can apply this technique by listing habits and goals and scheduling specific times for associated reward/routine behaviours each day. Checking off completions mentally contrasts this positive reward future with obstacles inhibiting the behaviour in the present. This motivates ensuring reaping later rewards while improving self-awareness of triggers hindering progress.

Frequent tracking keeps routines top-of-mind and convenient to implement without as much reliance on intrinsic self-discipline. Over time, habitual cues become automatically tied to targeted behaviours through consistent contrast of rewards and obstacles. Social accountability from sharing progress reinforces motivation when commitment may falter due to weaknesses in sustained self-determination, a characteristic of ADHD.

With regular use of tracking tools combining mental contrasts, healthy patterns are deliberately conditioned to accommodate inherent difficulties in spontaneous organisation for those affected by ADHD.

Ways to use habit trackers using the technique of mental contrasting:

List desired habits as goals down one column. Include columns for each day, and place a checkmark upon completion.

Write out positive future outcomes from consistently making the habit at the top, like having more free time or feeling pride in accomplishments.

Expect potential barriers that could interfere with each goal to acknowledge obstacles upfront.

Set reminders on your phone or calendar to prompt recording completion during natural routine times each day.

Physically check off boxes to tangibly contrast present success versus potential future failure without the habit.

Note the feelings of achievement experienced by tracking progress daily.

Review unchecked days to strategise overcoming future barriers through adjusted planning.

Share progress publicly to maintain accountability through social motivation when discipline wavers.

Reward tracking stretches weekly to envision and fulfil outcomes, continuously motivating the routine.

Gradually increase goals over time as habits automatically take hold through repetition and positive reinforcement.

Contingency planning against barriers and scheduled check-ins keeps routines top of-mind with ADHD through mental rehearsal of rewards.

Setting meaningful, trackable, and accomplishable goals is notoriously tricky for individuals with ADHD due to impairments in executive function. The SMART framework is an effective goal-setting structure that makes goal pursuit more concrete and supports sustained motivation.

SMART is an acronym for Specific, Measurable, Attainable, Realistic, and Timebound. These criteria help define goals in a clear, organised manner. Breaking ambitious targets into more minor, short-term SMART objectives is critical to success for those with ADHD.

Specific goals eliminate ambiguity by identifying what needs to be done. Vague, general goals are difficult to initiate without clear direction. Detailing out who, what, where, and when in SMART objectives provides the scaffolding to get started.

Its important goals are measurable by associating them with quantifiable metrics. Numbers add tangibility versus vagueness, making progress visible and avoiding assumptions on completion. Tracking metrics keeps named parties accountable.

Attainable yet challenging goals set the stage for achievement while avoiding feeling overwhelmed. Considering motivation, past performance, and limitations helps determine appropriate stretch targets.

Realism acknowledges obstacles inherent to goal circumstances and one's weaknesses. Overly optimistic timelines demotivate upon first impediment versus flexible targets adjusted as needed.

Lastly, establishing firm timelines in calendars maintains awareness and momentum versus loose ideas prone to deferral and abandonment. Telling reminders helps time-bound efforts feel urgent.

Setting and achieving goals can be challenging for those with ADHD due to impairments in executive functioning skills. The SMART framework provides an effective structure to break significant goals into smaller, more manageable tasks. The specifics of SMART goals:

Making goals Specific ensures they are unambiguous. Vague, general goals lack direction, which allows procrastination to set in quickly—detailing each small objectives who, what, where, and when provides the necessary scaffolding to get started. Concrete steps activate focus.

Also, goals are Measurable. Associating goals with quantitative metrics makes progress feel visible versus subjective guesses of completion. Numbers satisfy the dopamine-seeking nature of ADHD. Tracking metrics keeps one accountable and motivated.

Goals should be Attainable yet challenging enough to stimulate effort. Considering strengths, past performance, and limitations helps determine a suitable level of stretch. Meeting reasonable expectations builds confidence.

In addition, goals need to be Realistic, acknowledging potential obstacles or weaknesses inherent to the goal or the individual striving for it. Overly optimistic timelines risk demotivating at the first hurdle compared to flexible targets.

Finally, establishing Time-bound deadlines and due dates maintains organisation and momentum versus loose ideas prone to delay. Calendaring reminders create urgency.

Breaking the process into multiple, smaller SMART goals has more benefits for sustaining long-term motivation, a common challenge for those with ADHD.

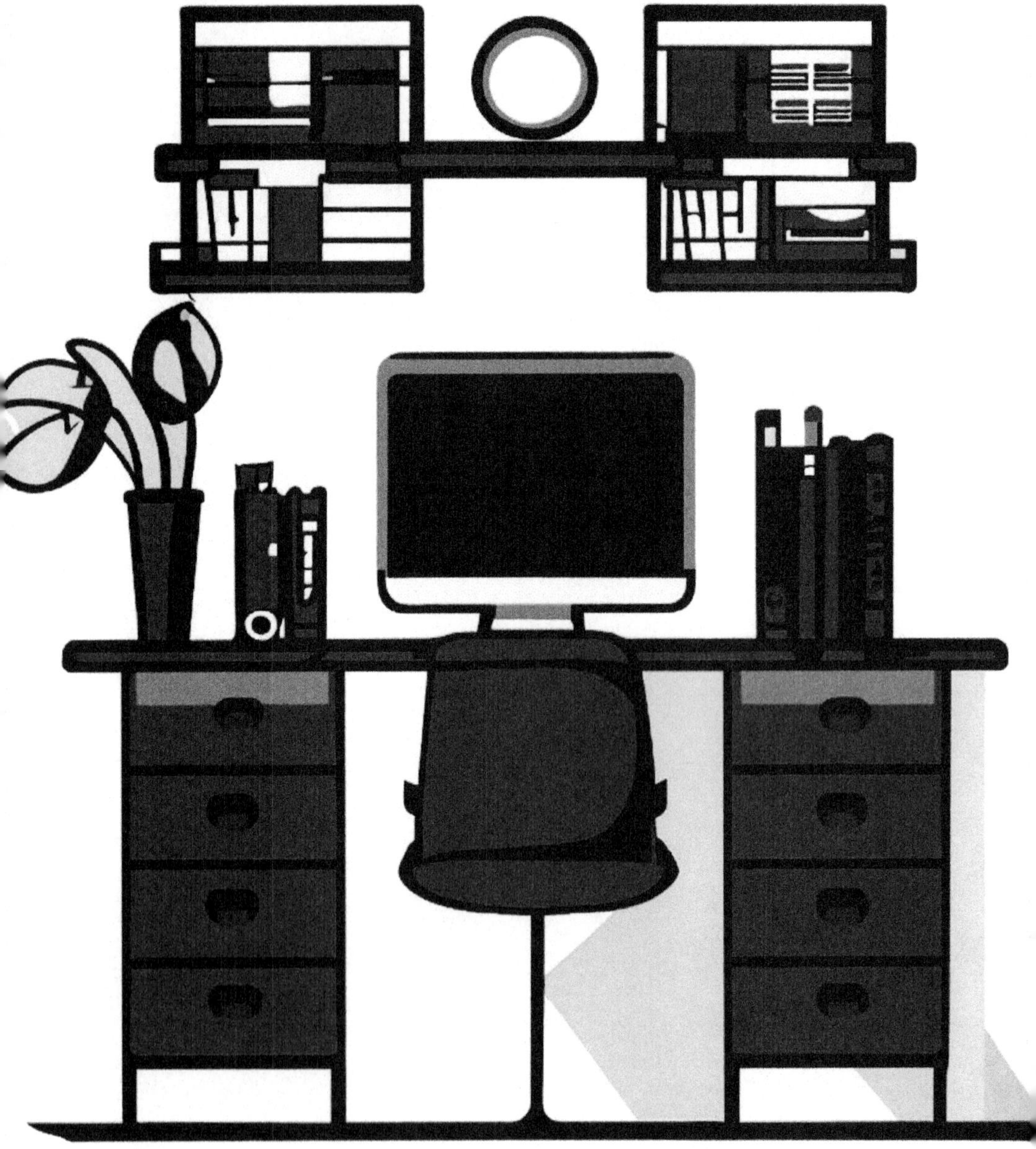

CHAPTER 7

Mastering Organisation

For individuals with ADHD, having an organised system is important for staying on top of responsibilities and managing distractibility. Yet, traditional planners and organisational methods often fail to accommodate the unique challenges of impaired executive function. This chapter will explore proven strategies for gaining control through customisation and digital tools.

Specific topics will include bullet journaling and novel notebook setups that spark motivation, step-by-step guides for decluttering and managing paperwork through intuitive filing systems, checklists for organising one's home and workspace, and recommendations for favourite apps that utilise friendly reminders and calendars.

By adopting organisational methods that leverage individual strengths while bypassing weaknesses, readers will walk away with effective personalised solutions for keeping information and environments well-ordered.

For those with ADHD, traditional planners and to-do lists often fail to sustain use over time due to a lack of adaptability and visual appeal. Bullet journaling provides a customisable solution that engages individuals through creative expression while maintaining structure. Bullet journals' open-ended, modular nature allows for a personalisation that prevents boredom - a critical downfall of more rigid systems. Elements like decorative spreads, tracking habits through visual cues, and inserting hobbies alongside responsibilities integrate effortless planning into an enjoyable process. This intrinsic motivation to regularly update and review journals boosts executive functioning abilities.

For those prone to losing focus or interest, bullet journaling supplies motivating short-term improvements to build long-term organisation skills. Above all, the flexibility to change layouts means individuals can tailor their journals precisely to the variations in attention and priorities common to ADHD.

Here are ideas for customising a bullet journal to work for those with ADHD:

Keep it simple - a notebook with monthly and daily logs is enough to avoid overwhelming.

Use thick, colourful markers and stickers for visually stimulating, satisfying entries.

Integrate art, doodles, and washi tape to customise spreads and stay engaged during planning.

Set up well-spaced monthly logs that leave room for checking tasks as complete with stamps or stickers.

Create weekly logs spread across two pages for adequate spacing of to-dos broken into time blocks.

Incorporate inspirational quotes, song lyrics, or photos that spark joy to maintain interest.

Label sections clearly with bold headers to quickly scan upcoming tasks and commitments.

Leave additional blank pages between sections to jot down fleeting thoughts or notes on the fly.

Experiment with minimalist or maximalist styles to see which fosters routine tracking most efficiently.

Change as needed by removing unused spreads or reformatting for busy periods to retain flexibility.

Staying on top of paperwork is challenging for many with ADHD due to difficulties with focus, follow-through, and executive function. Yet, an organised filing system is important for efficiently managing essential documents like bills, taxes, warranties, and medical records. A disordered paper pile invites stress, making paperwork hard to reference and promptly address. This increases the risk of late fees or missed deadlines. An intuitive folder structure tailored to individual needs can empower those with ADHD to gain control.

Here are tips for setting up effective folder categories:

Set up general folders for different types of paperwork. Commonly needed categories include bills, taxes, warranties, medical records, school documents, and finance records. Assign each a designated folder and colour for easy recognition.

Within each main folder, include labelled dividers to separate important subcategories further. For bills, for example, divide by a utility company or streaming service for quick retrieval.

Organise folders alphabetically or chronologically depending on the logical way to access the contents. Bills sorted alphabetically together may work better than chronologically mixed.

Designate a consistent home for the folder system, whether in a binder, vertical files, or storage cabinet/drawer. Keeping files together streamlines maintenance.

Consider digitising documents using scanning apps when possible. This allows searching for keywords for hard-to-find papers and backup protection in case of file loss.

Tips For Effective Long-Term Paperwork Management

Managing paperwork long-term requires effective systems to avoid clutter and ensure essential documents can easily be located later when needed. Here are helpful tips for maintaining organisational best practices over time:

Proper documentation, filing, and storage are essential for focus and peace of mind, but setting up sustainable systems requires ongoing effort. Developing routines like:

Set calendar reminders to regularly review and purge outdated documents based on a retention schedule. For example, shred tax documents after seven years.

Assign a flat workspace surface, such as shelves or desktop trays, to address incoming papers quickly before they pile up.

Back up essential documents digitally on an external hard drive or store copies off-site with a family member in an emergency.

Use colourful labels, sorting trays, or decorative binders to spark joy and visually incentivise the often-tedious filing process.

Consider starting each New Year or tax season with comprehensive paperwork cleanout and organisation refreshes.

Digitally file scanned receipts into labelled spreadsheets by year for ease of expense tracking if needed.

Involve family members, especially a supportive partner, in the mutual accountability of designated paperwork areas, staying neat and current.

By implementing a customised system tailored to individual needs and strengths, those with ADHD can experience long-term relief from the stress of unmanaged paperwork piles through increased organisation.

An organised home and workspace can help adults with ADHD manage their responsibilities and daily tasks. According to a 2014 study published in the journal Brain and Cognition, individuals with ADHD show impaired ability to sustain attention and focus due to deficits in executive function skills related to organisation and prioritisation. Researchers found that a disorganised physical environment exacerbates these challenges by overburdening limited cognitive resources.

Regular organisation through checklists is a proven strategy for offloading some of this mental workload. A 2012 study in the Journal of Attention Disorders showed establishing routines to routinely declutter living and working areas, with designated spots for everyday items, reduced cognitive distraction for participants with ADHD. With external structures in place, participants reported better maintaining focus without constant environmental decisions interfering.

More research has shown that checklists are an evidence-based memory aid. A 2020 study in the journal Memory compared the note-taking of college students with and without ADHD and found those with the disorder benefited far more significantly from detailed, step-by-step checklists to guide tasks than vague to-do lists—the tangible visual breakdown of activities in a checklist format allowed for greater ease in planning and execution.

Helping to minimise environmental distractions and providing a concrete structure for organisation efforts and home and workspace checklists can empower adults with ADHD to overcome cognitive processes like working memory impairments.

Following these proven routines sets the stage for more efficient daily functioning and a lower burden on limited executive functions that can impede independence and success.

Here are tips to include on checklists for organising the home and workspace:

Home Organisation Checklist

Staying organised at home and in the workspace is essential for maintaining focus and mental clarity. Thorough decluttering sessions throughout the year minimise distractions so limited attention can be devoted to critical tasks. Some practical tips to incorporate into checklists include:

Regularly reviewing and reorganising living and work environments boosts productivity. Checklists break down larger organisation goals into smaller, actionable steps like:

Declutter countertops, tables, desks and reduce visual clutter

Sort through the mail and shred unnecessary items

Organise paperwork and files into labelled binders

Clean out refrigerator and pantry, donating expired food

Purge the closet by consolidating seasons and donating unused items

Organise medications and supplements by time of day

Schedule deep cleaning tasks for rooms like bathrooms monthly

Workspace Organisation Checklist

An organised workspace is essential for maintaining focus and productivity. Work areas also require periodic deep cleaning and reorganisation, as with home living spaces. Some helpful tips to include in a checklist for decluttering the office or study area include:

In addition to regularly organising living spaces, tidy work environments are equally important for minimising mental distractions. An effective Workspace Organisation Checklist can facilitate sometimes purging non-essentials to stay concentrated on essential tasks. This includes actions such as:

Clean and clear desk surfaces of non-essential items

Sort supplies into labelled drawers and storage bins

Backup and purge computer files, removing unnecessary programs

Tidy bookshelves by category and size for aesthetics

Organise paperwork trays with labelled folders for projects

Maintain desk calendar and schedules in one centralised location

Charge devices in designated areas to avoid cluttered surfaces

Clean and disinfect electronics and work tools routinely

Checklists help declutter methodically and establish routines to maintain organisation for ideal focus and productivity. Tidy areas free of distractions set the stage for success.

However, relying on paper-based planners and filing systems often poses unique challenges for those with ADHD due to working memory deficits and difficulties with organisation. Digital organisation apps are specially designed to bypass these weaknesses through intuitive features like automatic reminders, cloud syncing across devices, and searchable note capabilities. This lets vital information be easily accessed without requiring perfect recall. Research has found such high-tech solutions can significantly bolster executive functioning for those with ADHD. Specific tools like calendar apps with notification settings, task managers broken into lists and due dates, and password managers that auto-generate secure credentials have proven effective at reducing cognitive load.

Here are ways digital organisation apps can help those with ADHD:

Calendar Apps

Calendar applications that sync across devices and send notifications can help individuals with ADHD stay on schedule. Google Calendar lets colour-coding events and customising views optimise organisation. Its advanced notification settings help prevent missed appointments. Outlook integrates well with other Microsoft tools and permits blocking out distraction-free focus periods. This ensures users face fewer interruptions when trying to concentrate.

Reminder Apps

Reminder apps provide automatic pop-ups to prevent task slippage. The Reminders app that comes standard with Apple devices allows location-based prompts, reminding users of errands or chores when they are near relevant stores. Todoist is a powerful task manager, letting users break large projects into smaller, more manageable nested subtasks assigned to customised due dates. Its robust functionality and device syncing keep details from falling through the cracks.

Note-Taking Apps

Evernote excels at housing many notes, documents, photos, and clippings in individually customisable notebooks. Its robust search and tagging capabilities make essential information easy to find later. OneNote by Microsoft also organises information across sections, pages, and laptops while allowing the embedding of files, web clips, and audio/video recordings. The search tool and cloud syncing across devices ensure consistency.

Password Managers

Password manager apps generate unique, strong passwords and auto-fill login credentials on websites, taking the mental load off users. Popular options like LastPass and 1Password securely store all website account information in digital vaults accessible with master passwords or fingerprints for convenience.

By offloading organisational demands, digital solutions empower those with ADHD to streamline daily tasks through intuitive, accessible features optimised for the distracted mind. Proper setup tailors assistance to individual needs.

Various paper-based and digital systems can help individuals with ADHD stay organised and on top of daily responsibilities and paperwork. Bullet journaling was presented as a customisable planner option that allows for tracking schedules, tasks, and habits creatively and visually stimulatingly. Tips were given for adapting bullet journals to work effectively for those with attention deficits.

Establishing intuitive filing systems was emphasised, with suggestions like colour-coding folders and including dividers. Maintaining digital backups of important documents provides more protection. Calendaring and reviewing deadlines prevent late fees or missed opportunities.

Having designated home spaces for incoming mail, files, and active projects aids in timely processing instead of piles taking over. Decluttering and purging on a routine schedule are also essential. Involving an accountability partner can also support organisational upkeep.

Digital tools that provide structure through reminders, cloud storage, and search functions were highlighted as particularly beneficial for ADHD working memory challenges. Specific apps for calendar management, task tracking, notes, bills, and passwords were outlined.

Customised paper and tech solutions that engage the distracted mind through intuitive features, such as reminders and visual design elements, can empower ADHD survivors to gain control over daily responsibilities through improved organisational skills.

Resilience

ADHD

Survivor's Note

I know that organisation does not come naturally to you, but please don't lose hope. Remember that you have incredible creativity and unique perspectives to offer the world. While organisation may seem tedious at times, finding systems that work for you will open up more space in your mind for all your great ideas to take shape. Be patient and kind with yourself as you experiment with planners, checklists, and filing methods. It may take some trial and error to discover what clicks. And it's okay if things slip - every slight improvement moves you closer to your goals.

Focus on small, manageable wins each day rather than perfection. Celebrate the progress you are making to tame distractions and take control. I have faith that your determination and problem-solving skills will serve you well on this journey. You've got this. Your brilliant heart and spirit are far more critical than any messy desk. Keep rediscovering what inspires that spark within as you learn. I believe in you and cannot wait to see all the fantastic things you'll continue to create with your mind fully liberated.

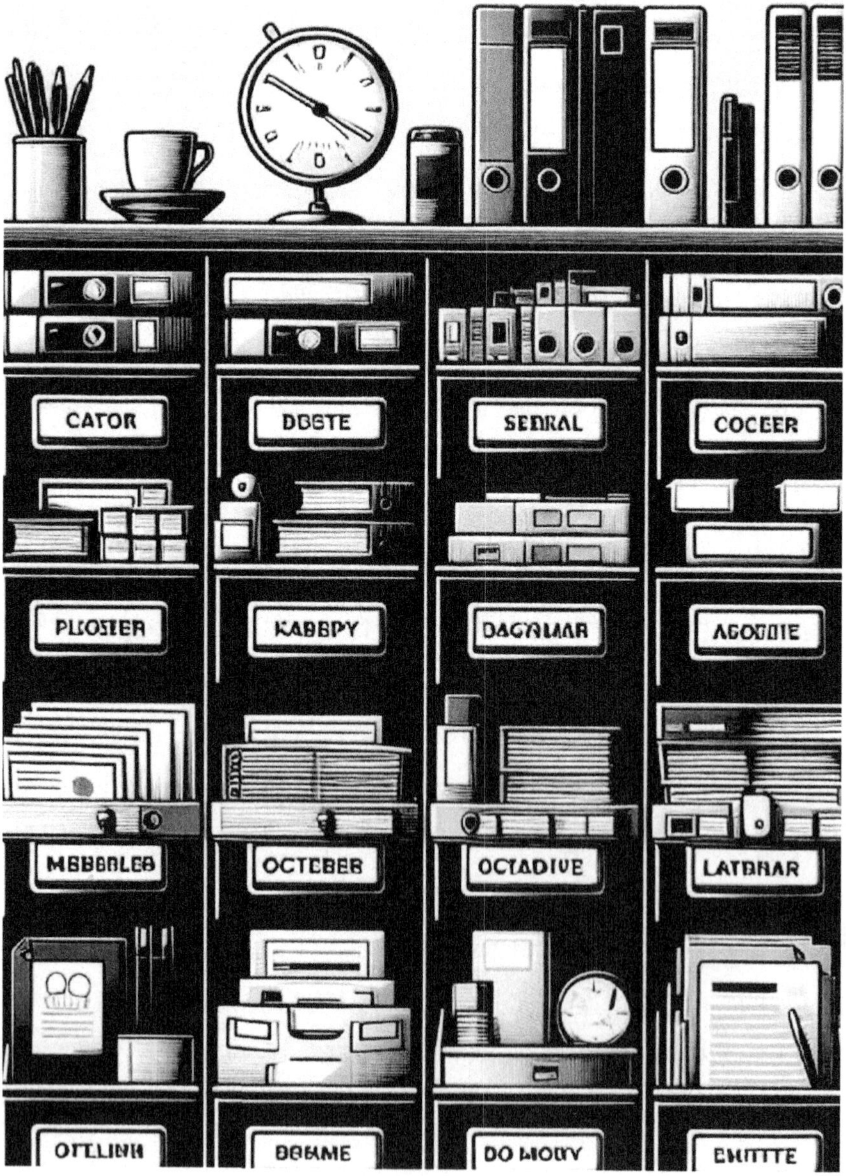
CATOR
COCEER
OCTEBER
OCTADIVE
LATBRAR

CHAPTER 8

Managing Emotion

Emotional regulation can present unique challenges for those who have learned to thrive despite the challenges of attention deficit hyperactivity disorder (ADHD). As multiple scientific studies have found, individuals with ADHD show reduced activation in prefrontal brain regions associated with executive functions during emotional processing tasks. This lower prefrontal cortex activity, as shown in a 2010 functional MRI study published in the Archives of General Psychiatry, means emotions may feel more intense and overwhelming for those with ADHD, making modulation difficult.

However, with self-awareness and the practice of effective strategies, ADHD survivors are empowered to gain increasing control over their emotional experiences. This chapter will explore the connection between ADHD and emotional dysregulation from a scientific and practical perspective while providing tools grounded in research to identify, express, and process feelings constructively. As survivors continue honing skills central to living successfully with neurodiversity, such as cognitive flexibility and emotional maturity, they bolster resilience and strengthen relationships.

As anyone living with attention deficit hyperactivity disorder knows well, executive function impairments from the condition can translate to difficulties regulating responses to both internal emotional experiences and external triggers that provoke distress. While popular perceptions of ADHD often focus only on hyperactive behaviours, an equally important aspect is the impact on emotional control and well-being. Gaining awareness of the neurological links between ADHD and emotion regulation is an important first step toward empowering survivors to advocate for their emotional health.

With understanding comes compassion for the self and tools to short-circuit unproductive tendencies and cultivate resilient coping. This chapter aims to provide that scientific foundation and set of techniques supporting ADHD survivors in transforming a perceived weakness into yet another pathway of personal growth and strength.

Here are key points about the association between ADHD and emotional regulation challenges:

The prefrontal cortex, responsible for executive functions like impulse control and cognitive flexibility, is essential in modulating emotional responses.

Research has found that individuals with ADHD have reduced activation in prefrontal brain regions involved in emotion regulation. This includes a functional MRI study published in 2010.

Decreased prefrontal activity means emotions may feel more intense and overwhelming for those with ADHD, making regulation difficult.

ADHD has also been linked to higher sensitivity to emotional stimuli through neuroimaging research.

Common challenges with emotional regulation seen in ADHD include difficulty identifying emotions, intense emotional reactions, struggles to shift attention away from distressing feelings, impulsive expressions of emotion without considering consequences, and rumination on negative emotions.

Executive functions impaired in ADHD, such as working memory, organisation, time management, and flexibility, are also critical skills for regulating emotional responses.

A meta-analysis published in 2013 showed ADHD to be significantly associated with deficits in general emotion regulation abilities compared to non-ADHD controls.

Enhanced regulation strategies are particularly important for those with ADHD to cope effectively, have relationships, and function optimally under pressure or distress.

Recognising and constructively communicating one's emotions is essential for well-being and building solid relationships. However, research shows this can be a particular challenge for those living with ADHD. Studies using EEG and fMRI technology have found that individuals with ADHD show decreased activity in the prefrontal cortex during tasks involving emotional recognition and processing (Burgess et al., 2010; Hutcherson et al., 2018). This brain region is important in identifying feelings and modulating expressive responses. Additionally, neuroimaging research has linked ADHD to heightened amygdala reactivity when exposed to emotional stimuli. The amygdala triggers autonomic arousal, contributing to more intense feelings and difficulties regulating reactions for those affected. So developing self-awareness and adaptive expression of emotions is essential to ADHD self-management. The following section will explore practical strategies grounded in science for identifying internal states and productively sharing feelings with others. Over time, these skills empower survivors to advocate for their mental wellness.

Here are some tips for identifying and expressing feelings in more detail:

Learn Self-Awareness of Bodily Sensations

Pay attention to how different emotions manifest physically in your body. Familiar sensations for various emotions include tightness in the chest for anxiety, upset stomach for stress/worry, and tension in the shoulders/jaw for anger. Keeping a diary to note sensations and connected feelings can help build awareness.

Use Feelings Checklists

Referring to an emotions checklist that outlines common feelings words can help you better understand and label what you may be experiencing physically. Checklists also present options to consider if you're unsure how to describe a new or complex sensation.

Open Communication

When sharing how you feel with others, try to provide context for what triggered the emotion and be specific about the physical sensations and thoughts connected to the feeling state. Example: "My heart started racing when you said X because, in my mind, it brought up worries about Y."

Expressing Strong Emotions

If you are upset, take deep breaths and remove yourself from the immediate situation before trying to have a constructive dialogue. Return when you've calmed down so you can listen and communicate respectfully.

"I feel..." Statements

To properly take ownership, start descriptions of your emotional experience with "I feel..." rather than accusatory language. For example, say, "I feel hurt when you do X," not "You hurt me by doing X."

Develop Empathy

Try imagining specifically what emotions another person involved may be feeling in a situation based on their likely perspective. Reflecting these back can strengthen understanding.

Physical Release

When feeling highly distressed, engage in calming sensory activities like drawing, knitting, or using clay. Exercising like running can also help diffuse built-up emotions over time.

Deep Breathing

Consciously control your breathing to lower activation in the sympathetic nervous system and "flip the switch" in the prefrontal cortex back to a calmer state for clearer thinking.

Challenge Thoughts

Question irrational beliefs that may intensify emotions and consider alternate perspectives that could help reframe reactions in a less distressing light.

While developing self-awareness of emotions and healthy expression are essential skills, managing feelings the moment they arise is equally important for well-being. This is where relaxation and adaptive coping mechanisms prove invaluable. However, research has shown that individuals with ADHD face more hurdles in using regulation strategies due to impairments in executive functioning (Miller et al., 2013). The impulsivity and difficulty with delaying gratification associated with ADHD can inhibit the implementation of calming practices effectively. So survivors must have a "toolbox" filled with evidence-based techniques that match their strengths. The following section will outline specific relaxation and coping strategies proven to help ADHD-affected individuals feel collected during distressing times. Regular practice is important in building resilience and making emotional competence a reality, even in life's most challenging moments.

Managing stress, anxiety, and negative emotions is essential for cognitive performance and well-being. While relaxation looks different for everyone, successful coping strategies promote calm focus. Here are some evidence-based options to experiment with:

Our mental state significantly affects cognitive function, so intentionally reducing stress is important. These techniques calmly redirect rampant thoughts while soothing the nervous system.

Here are some of the relaxation and coping strategies in more detail:

Deep Breathing: Inhale through your nose for 5 seconds, feeling your belly rise, then exhale slowly through pursed lips for 7 seconds. Repeat until you feel calmer.

Progressive Muscle Relaxation: Starting with your toes, tense each muscle group (feet, calves, thighs, etc.) for 5 seconds, then relax and feel the tension for 30 seconds. Work your way through all major muscle groups.

Guided Imagery: Find a short, calming script online to follow along with daily. For example, envision standing on a quiet beach, listening to waves, and feeling the soft sand between your toes.

Grounding Techniques: Sit in a comfortable spot and slowly note 5 things you see, four things you feel, three things you hear, two things you smell, and one thing you taste. Repeat as needed.

Soothing Baths: Draw a warm bath, light candles, play relaxing music, and soak for 20 minutes while reading or practising deep breathing.

Expressive Arts: Keep creative materials on hand and work through intense emotions through drawing, painting, poetry, etc., without judgment on artistic ability.

Exercise: Aim for 30 minutes daily of an activity you enjoy, like walking, jogging, yoga, or dancing, that lets you sweat and better process stress.

Nature: Spend 15-30 minutes outside, noticing simple pleasures like temperature, skies, plants, and animals to refresh your mind and spirit.

Talk to Others: Share how you're feeling with understanding friends/family or a therapist to gain new outlooks and feel supported during upsets.

Cognitive Restructuring: Note thoughts fuelling distress, then deliberately think of alternatives and how beliefs affect mood in session workbooks.

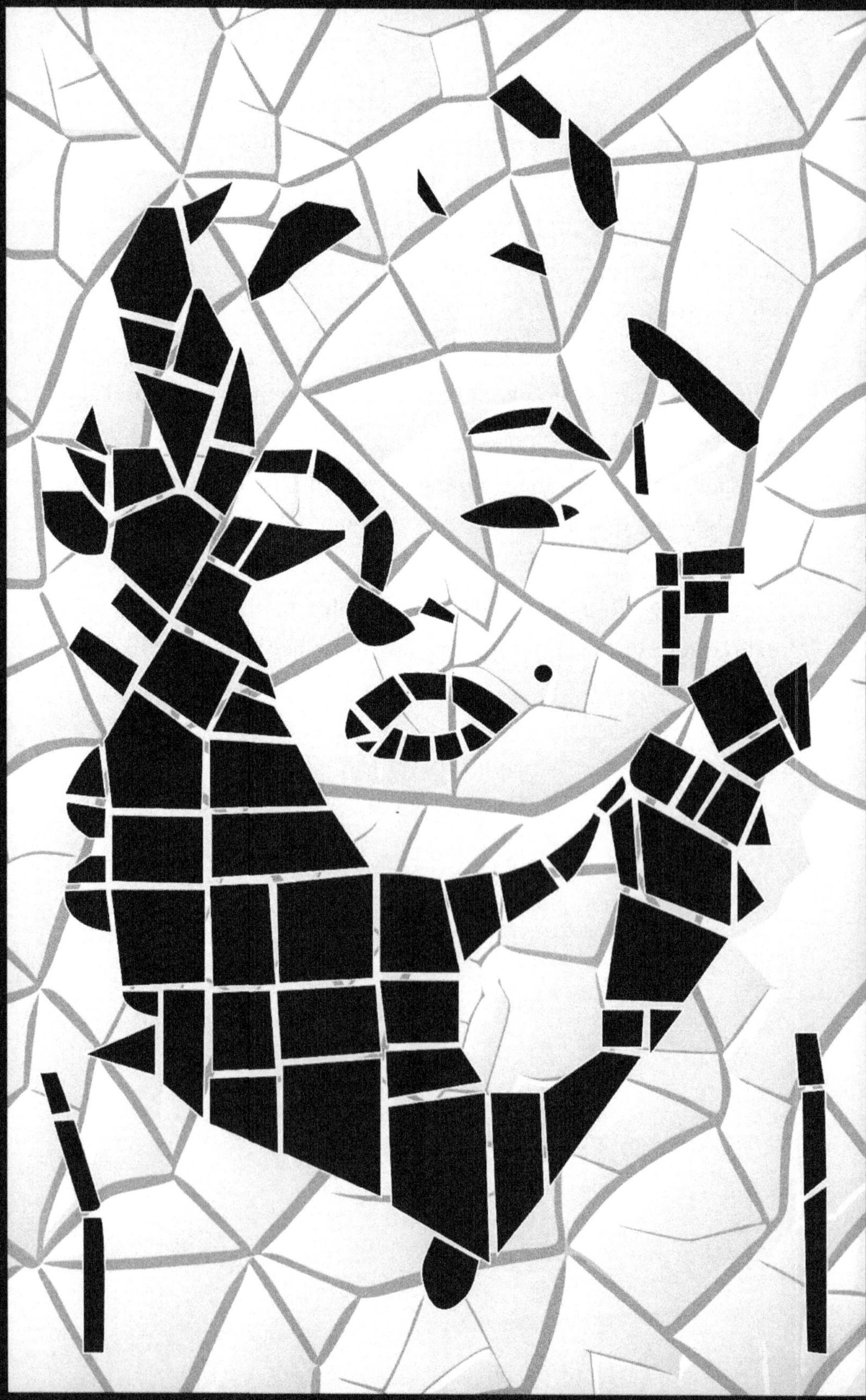

Survivor's Note

Each day presents new challenges as we navigate life with neurodiversity. Emotional regulation may not come naturally, but through self-reflection and strategy development, we are empowering ourselves. Though this journey brings frustration, never forget how far you've come.

Remember that frustrations are obstacles to work through, not barriers that define us. We can strategise to boost focus and manage distractions. We can visualise success to fortify motivation during setbacks. We can empathise with ourselves through difficulties instead of harsh self-criticism.

While the neurotypical world may not always understand our struggles, within our community lies deep wisdom of perseverance. We support each other not through absolutes but compassion. We celebrate persistence over perfection.

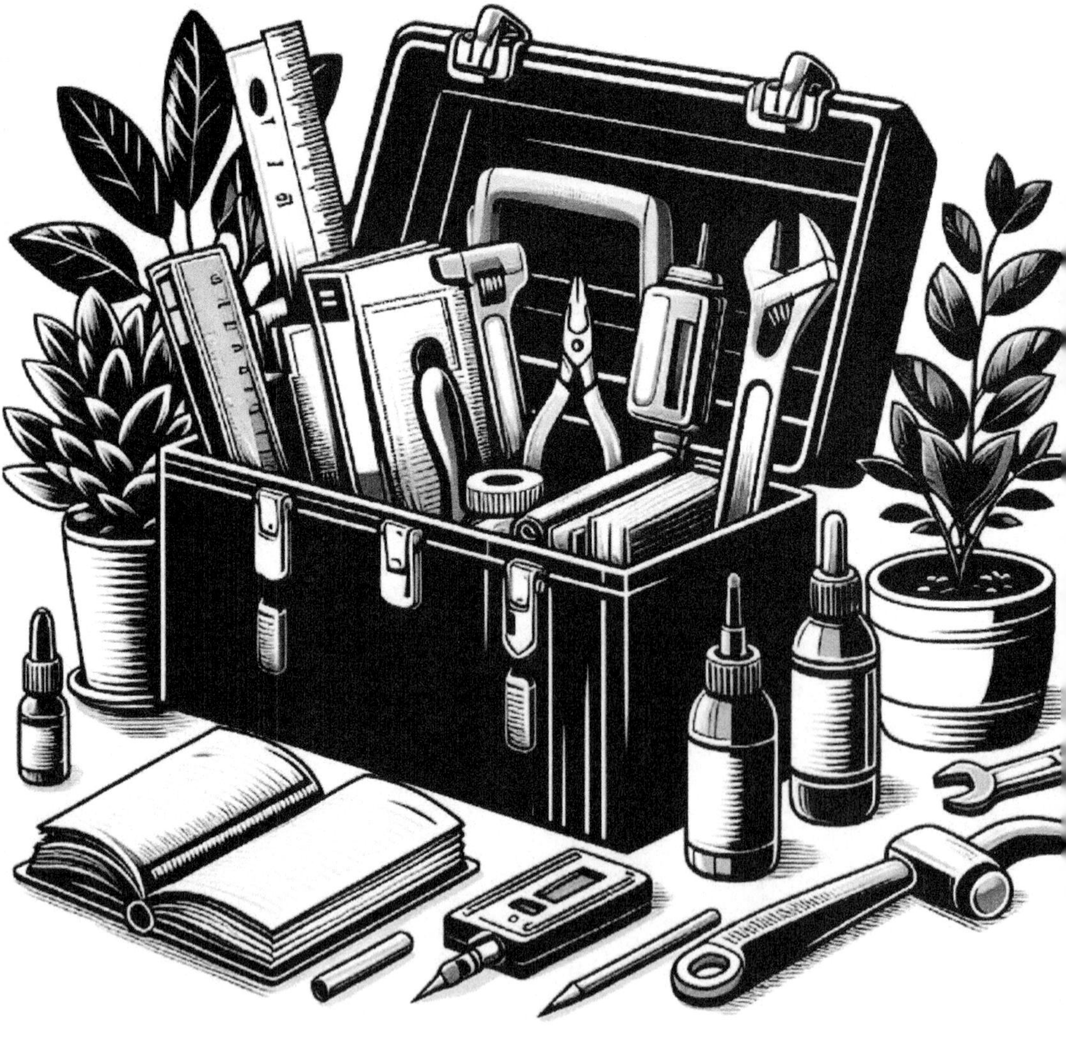

CHAPTER 9

Developing Coping Strategies

Now that we have explored the neuroscientific links between ADHD and emotional regulation challenges and discussed various techniques for identifying and processing feelings, it is time to dig deeper into developing a customised set of coping strategies. As with any skill, learning effective emotional regulation takes dedicated practice tailored to individual needs and strengths.

This chapter will provide a framework for building resilience through adaptive coping mechanisms that play to the capabilities of those with ADHD. We will outline the importance of experimenting to discover what works best in different scenarios and committing strategies to consistent practice until they become habits. Supporting emotional competence requires patience, flexibility, and compassion - both with oneself and in support of fellow survivors.

By gaining awareness of triggers, acknowledging limitations compassionately, and committing to personal wellness, ADHD-affected individuals can experience greater fulfilment and life satisfaction. Effectively coping with daily stresses, frustrations, and inner turmoil allows space to appreciate life's gifts. Let us embark on a journey of empowerment by cultivating a personalised arsenal of techniques for navigating challenges and celebrating victories, large or small, along the way.

For those with ADHD, coping with challenges to focus, persistence, and impulse control is often important for success across life domains. Whether in academic, professional, or personal contexts, environmental and internal distractions pose significant hurdles if not proactively managed. Multitasking abilities are usually overestimated, further exacerbating time management struggles. Heightened impulsivity can negatively affect essential decisions and relationships. Developing personalised strategies that promote sustained attention despite obstacles, minimise rushed behaviours, and satisfy fidgety urges in healthy ways is crucial to resilience for ADHD-affected individuals. These tips provide a starting point for experimenting with adaptive techniques tailored to an individual's strengths, limitations, and routines. Putting strategies into practice consistently and compassionately allows gradual progress toward emotional competence even when distraction-prone.

Here are some tips for managing distractions, multitasking, and impulsivity in more detail:

Remove Distractions

When studying, put your phone in a separate room or use silent notifications. Use browser extensions to block distracting sites for 30 minutes at a time. Close any other open tabs or programs on your computer that may divert attention.

Break Tasks into Steps

For a paper, list the sections/subheadings first and then fill in the details of each part one at a time. Taking brief breaks between sections can help maintain focus.

Use a Timer

Set a Pomodoro-style timer for 25 minutes of uninterrupted focus, then take a 5-minute break and repeat.

Declutter Your Space

Keep what's essential on your desk - put extra items in drawers so the surroundings are simple.

Limit Multitasking

If you are watching TV, don't check your phone. Complete one task before moving to the next.

Checklists & Reminders

Make checklists for daily routines, classes, and appointments to reference. Set calendar reminders.

Pause Before Acting

When you feel anger/impulse coming on, excuse yourself. Count to 100 slowly to cool down.

Find Movement Outlets

Keep a stress ball, doodle on paper, or quickly walk around the block when your body feels antsy.

Exercise Daily

Aim for 30 minutes of activity like running, sports, or yoga to release energy and better focus after.

Prioritise Sleep

Consistently going to bed and waking at set times helps manage fatigue that fuels impulsivity.

Celebrate Small Wins

Give self-praise for finishing just one section of an assignment to boost motivation.

Managing emotions effectively requires understanding feelings and relaxation skills and adapting to problems that provoke distressing states. Those with ADHD face particular hurdles with issues that demand sustained attention, organisation, and delayed decision-making. However, with practice deploying structured approaches, problems become growth opportunities rather than overwhelming roadblocks. Learning to break down difficulties into smaller pieces, brainstorming multiple solutions objectively, tracking patterns over time, and leveraging support enable problem-solving prowess closely linked to resilience and well-being. These strategies offer a starting point for methodically navigating challenging circumstances and developing this essential lifelong coping competence.

Breaking down significant problems into smaller, more manageable pieces can help avoid overwhelming problems. Examine the components of an overarching issue and prioritise which to tackle first. Addressing problems step-by-step makes enduring setbacks feel more surmountable. Keeping a journal or calendar to track setbacks, frustrations, and potential causes over time helps identify patterns. Noting circumstances, mindsets, or activities preceding struggles provides insight into root issues. With awareness of patterns comes empowerment to make changes, reducing future difficulties.

Brainstorming multiple potential solutions without judgment generates many options to consider. Write down all ideas, however improbable, to widen your perspective. Later, critically and objectively weighing the pros and cons of each alternative reveals possible approaches warranting experimentation.

Consulting how others have solved similar problems can trigger fresh ideas when feeling stuck. Contacting trusted peers or professionals taps into diverse experiences of overcoming adversity. When upset or biased thinking clouds objective reasoning, an outside viewpoint also provides an anchoring sense of reality.

Trying temporary solutions allows for evaluating whether an approach helps somewhat while continuing the search for a long-term answer. Even a provisional fix offering slight relief buys time and motivation to address core problems thoroughly. This persevering attitude models that challenges are navigable through adaptation. Celebrating effort and small wins rather than only results strengthen resilience over time. With difficulty comes growth, so permitting experience alongside patience with self and situation cultivates a problem-solving practice, bringing ever greater calm and control.

Navigating setbacks, mistakes, failures, and interpersonal difficulties is an inevitable part of life. For those with ADHD, rejection sensitivity can amplify the emotional impact of stressful events like underperforming on an exam, not securing a desired job offer after interviews, or facing criticism from others. However, fostering resilience - the ability to adapt well in the face of adversity, trauma, tragedy, threats, or significant sources of stress - is critical to long-term well-being and success.

Building tolerance for anxiety, discomfort, or embarrassment associated with challenges takes ongoing effort tailored to individual experiences. For example, public speaking anxieties may be addressed differently than coping with a messy separation. Learning self-compassion helps reframe challenging interactions, from conflict with a parent to lack of acceptance into a selective program, as opportunities rather than proof of unworthiness. Developing resilience requires acknowledging distress while gaining perspective through strategies such as reframing negative self-talk, maintaining supportive relationships, engaging in meaningful activities, and celebrating small wins - even just completing an application or having the courage to try. These tips provide a starting point.

Reframe Mistakes

View errors as data, not debits. Note what you learned from a failed test, project, etc. How can you apply insights next time?

Normalise Stress

A racing heart or upset stomach when nervous is temporary and part of staying alert in a challenging situation. Deep breathing can help calm the body's reaction.

Feel Disappointment Without Catastrophising

Give yourself time to be sad about a rejection without assuming it means you're unworthy or successes are impossible. Remind yourself of other skills and opportunities.

Accept External Factors

Know the decision wasn't entirely in your hands. Don't personalise it or waste energy on "what ifs." Refocus on controllable things like your next steps.

Maintain Supportive People

Spend time with those who build you up without judgment. Know it's okay to come to them when discouraged to gain perspective in overcoming difficulties.

Positive Self-Talk

When anxious, replace harsh statements like "I can't do this" with kinder phrases such as "I will take it one step at a time" or "This feels scary, but I survived the last hard time and will get through this too."

Engage in Meaningful Activities

Pursuing hobbies provides enjoyment, purpose, and outlets for stress, whether sports, art, volunteering, or more. Commit to them for periodic breaks from demands.

Celebrate Perseverance

To stay motivated through setbacks, give credit where it's due by recognising each small success or effort rather than only focusing on the outcome.

Take Strategic Breaks

If overwhelmed, step away briefly, but plan to re-engage productively versus permanently avoid without first trying everything reasonable.

Remember, Stress/Rejection Are Part of Growth

View challenging experiences as part of strengthening resilience over the long haul rather than threats to be avoided at all costs by quitting before exhausting available options.

In this chapter, we have explored many coping strategies and techniques that can be helpful for individuals with ADHD in building emotional resilience. We discussed the importance of identifying triggers and processing feelings through journaling or discussion. To better manage stress, a framework was provided for experimenting with relaxation methods like deep breathing, meditation, physical activity, and mindfulness. Developing the ability to break considerable challenges into smaller, more manageable pieces allows for systematic problem-solving. Tips centred around managing distractions, limiting multitasking, and pausing before acting impulsively can boost focus and productivity. Building acceptance of stress and rejection as everyday life experiences was also covered. Maintaining supportive relationships, reframing setbacks positively, and celebrating effort promotes persistence through difficulties. The goal has been to outline a start to developing a personalised toolkit tailored to an individual's strengths to aid competent navigation of daily frustrations, and long-term life stresses with confidence, self-compassion, and fulfilment.

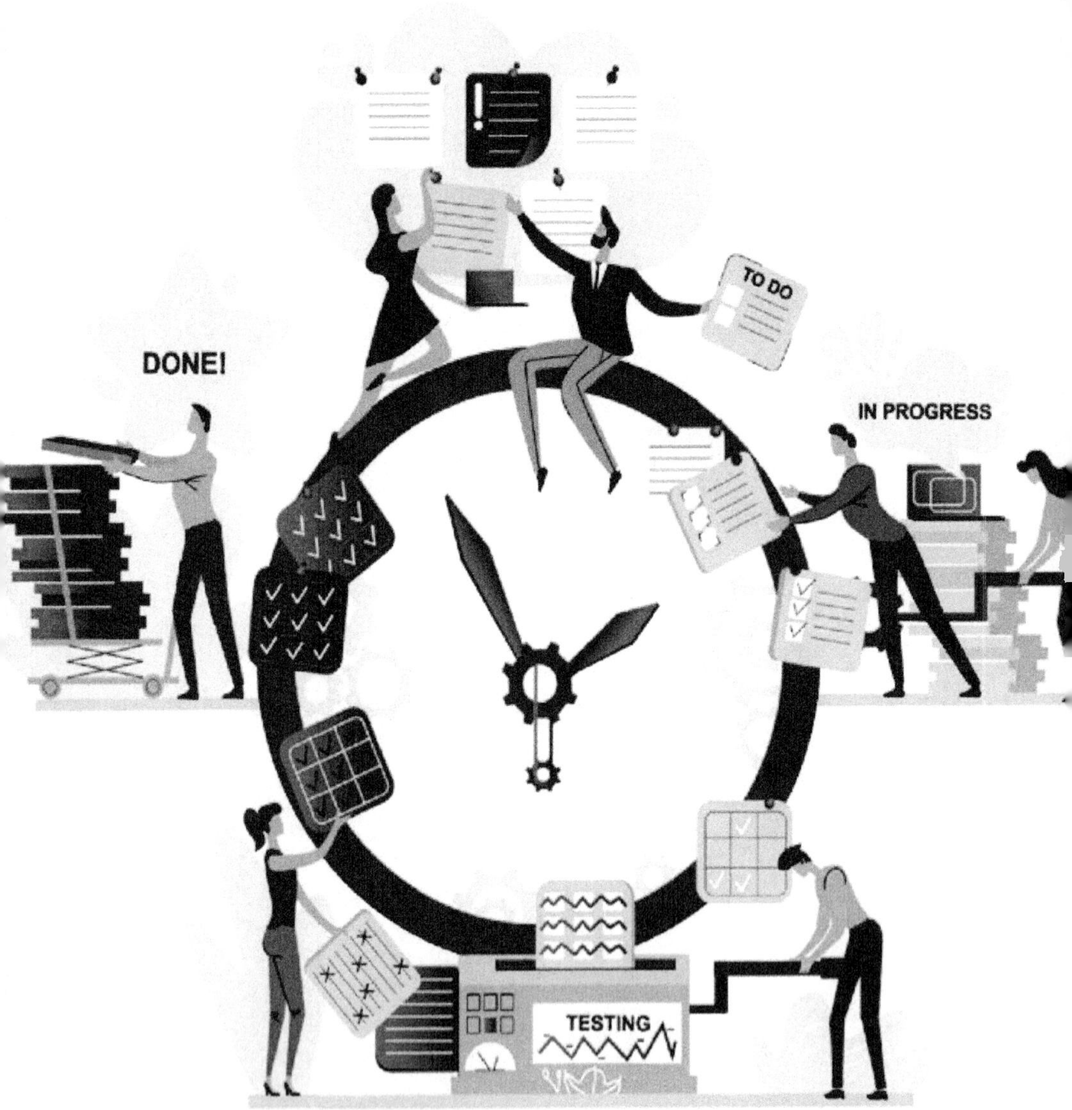
TO DO
DONE!
IN PROGRESS
TESTING

CHAPTER 10

Maintaining Routines and Consistency

Establishing and sustaining healthy habits and routines can be a significant challenge for many with ADHD due to impairments in self-regulation and impulse control. However, developing reliable structures and consistent daily practices is critical for emotional well-being, academic success, and optimal workplace functioning. This chapter will explore strategies for overcoming the struggle with maintaining routines, focusing on incorporating flexibility to accommodate neurodivergence. We will discuss techniques for problem-solving breakdowns and staying accountable through supportive systems. The goal is to provide a foundation for engineering an individualised approach to daily living that enhances balance and productivity over the long term, even during stress, transition, or overload on executive functions. Consistency takes patience and practice but yields lasting rewards of stability and confidence.

Involve dopamine-boosting tasks into your daily schedule to increase motivation and consistency in maintaining routines. Schedule preferred activities such as a favourite hobby, social media time, or video games after completing specific responsibilities.

Block off dedicated periods in the morning and evening specifically for self-care, relaxation, and winding down from the day's demands. This helps curb burnout and transition smoothly between work and personal modes. A similar block of downtime should be planned for weekends.

Planning meals and snacks throughout the day supports focus, energy levels, and adherence to routines. Prepare and pack sure snacks for specific times, like midmorning and after school/work. Routines also involve grocery shopping to keep healthy options stocked.

Including both cardiovascular exercise and shorter physical activity breaks in daily schedules provides many cognitive and emotional benefits. For example, a routine could involve daily walks outside or fitness classes twice a week. Even short movement breaks help circulation and creative problem-solving.

To avoid conflicts or double-booking, use a calendar to schedule commitments like classes, meetings, appointments, social plans, and chores/errands. Schedule some unstructured personal time and social engagements to promote balance and enjoyment of routines.

Allow specific periods of flexibility in routines and schedules for spontaneous activities as needed, unexpected events or changes to planned durations of particular tasks as realistic time estimates are established through experience. Rigid full schedules leave no room for this adaptability.

Routines become healthier and more consistent when collaboratively developed with family members or roommates and supported by each other through accountability. Communicate schedules and agree to check-ins or prompting as needed.

Gradually build routines over weeks and months by starting with just one or two small, manageable habits and schedules before layering on more structure. Introducing too much at once leads to quicker burnout.

Labelled storage spaces and supplies dedicated to each routine, such as school backpacks, fitness clothes drawers, and cooking ingredients areas, help people stick to schedules through visual organisation.

Using phone reminders, habit-tracking apps, checklists, and recurring alarms increases self-discipline through accountability. Review the weekly schedule and note what's working well and areas needing readjustment.

Celebrating successes, even tiny wins like making breakfast three days a week maintains motivation for continually improving routines through challenges and accomplishments over the long term. Progress is nonlinear and requires continued support through self-compassion.

For those with ADHD, busy or high-stress periods at work or school can overwhelm executive functioning skills and easily disrupt carefully crafted routines. However, maintaining some structure is essential for both productivity and mental well-being. Scaling back routines temporarily avoids frustration from taking on too much.

Sticking to core habits like regular meals and proper sleep provides stability when juggling multiple demands. This helps sustain the focus and energy needed to get through busy seasons. Enlisting accountability partners can motivate adhering to at least one or two priorities, like an important project.

Using rewards keeps routines engaging and helps reinforce positive behaviour during low dopamine or willpower. Things like a preferred snack or 10 minutes of leisure time provide motivation. Scheduling relaxation prevents burnout.

Prepping ahead saves valuable cognitive bandwidth otherwise spent on daily decisions and tasks. Simplifying cleaning and organisation further lightens the mental load.

Being kind and flexible with yourself prevents discouragement if routines must remain scaled back longer than expected due to unforeseen crunches. Persevering with even one daily routine reinforces structure.

Reaching out for support maintains emotional well-being when discipline with routines feels challenging. Balancing is critical—prioritising a few core routines preserves stability and confidence while respecting limits during demanding seasons.

Progress happens gradually through experiences.

Here are tips for sustaining discipline with routines during busy periods:

Scale back expectations and non-essential routines/schedules temporarily rather than feeling overwhelmed.

Stick to core habits like sleep, meal prep, and exercise to maintain health/focus.

If you are experiencing a temporary lull in self-motivation, ask others to help hold you accountable to 1-2 priorities.

Use a rewards system for sticking to scaled-down routines during bursts of busyness and productivity.

Schedule relaxing activities to prevent burnout when days are jam-packed.

Prep large batches of meals/snacks to save time and energy during hectic weeks. Keep supplies organised in clear areas to minimise decision fatigue.

Temporarily simplify schedules if routines begin slipping and reinstate thoroughly once pressures decrease.

Be patient and accepting versus discouraged if scaled-back routines must continue longer than expected.

Reach out for emotional support managing workloads through outlets like journaling or talking with understanding friends/family.

Avoid all-or-nothing thinking by preserving one or two routines, even on the most chaotic days. Consistency builds over time.

Focus on celebrations for routines maintained versus frustration over temporary diversions from ideal structures.

Routines can be a challenge for those with ADHD due to impairments in self-regulation and executive functioning. However, research shows developing consistency provides benefits like enhanced organisation, productivity, emotional well-being, and stress management. Because ADHD is a lifelong neurodevelopmental condition, routines also need ongoing improvement over time to accommodate changing needs, seasons of life, and levels of responsibilities Barkley (2021). This chapter will discuss why a continuous improvement mindset is important for ADHD survivors seeking to sustain healthy routines. Rather than stressing rigid structures, we'll cover a flexible and experiment-based approach proven to support routine adherence for the long haul through patience and persistence McDonald & Sarmiento (2022). Embracing small failures as feedback keeps routines engaging versus discouraging. A growth orientation cultivates routines that empower versus overwhelm.

Here are tips for taking a continuous improvement approach to developing and sustaining routines over time:

Review routines weekly or bi-weekly to evaluate what's working well versus areas needing change. Note tasks that consistently feel overwhelming.

Discuss routines regularly with an accountability partner, therapist, or coach to get an outside perspective on strengths and opportunities.

Gradually challenge yourself by adding a new routine component or levelling an existing habit in small increments.

Celebrate routine successes but also view slip-ups neutrally as feedback on what's realistic. Be willing to modify with compassion.

Use habit-tracking apps to track routine consistency over months to spot patterns requiring revised strategies.

Stay open to new organisational tools, techniques, or resources that could enhance routine setup and maintenance.

Expect routines to evolve along with changing needs, seasons, and life stages. Routines will not look the same years from now.

Persist through setbacks without harsh self-criticism by refocusing on overall progress versus former struggles.

Frame routines as ongoing experiments requiring flexibility rather than permanent blueprints. Commit to the Process.

Recognise small wins each week or month to fuel motivation for continual, gradual improvements toward personal goals.

The approach supports dynamic vs. rigid routines by embracing learning, adaptation, and incremental progress over quick fixes or perfection. Change happens through patience and persistence.

This chapter explains why developing routines is challenging for individuals with ADHD but essential for emotional regulation, productivity, and overall well-being. Critical strategies for creating initial schedules and routines are presented, including establishing dopamine-inducing habits, planning self-care time, exercising, and using technology for accountability. Tips for sustaining routines during busy periods through scaling back expectations and prepping meals are also shared.

Adopting a continuous improvement approach to routines rather than striving for rigid structures was discussed. A review process and discussing routines with others help identify strengths and areas for modification. Gradual challenges and celebrating wins support progression. Tracking progress over months allows for spotting patterns needing revised strategies.

Research showing the benefits of consistency for those with ADHD, such as enhanced organisation and stress management, was also referenced. Because ADHD is lifelong, routines must evolve with changing responsibilities and life stages through flexibility and patience. Framing routines as ongoing experiments cultivates a growth mindset that cultivates empowerment versus overwhelm in the face of inconsistency. This chapter's evidence-based practices will be a foundation for long-term routine success.

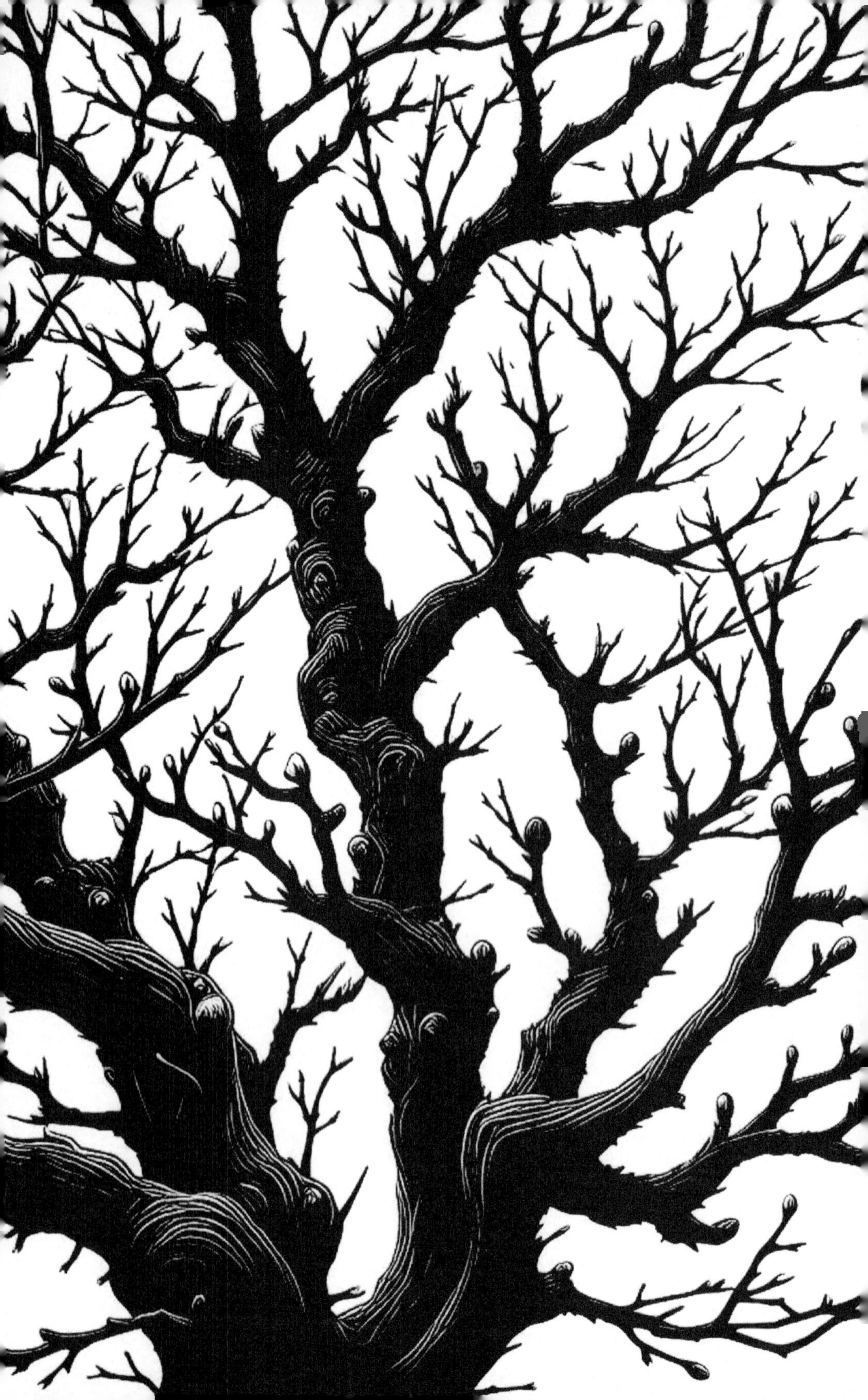

Survivor's Note

I know how difficult establishing and sustaining routines can feel with our ADHD brains. It's easy to get discouraged when the structure falls apart, even with the best intentions. Please remember that consistency is a process, not a perfect end goal. Each small win of sticking to a habit, each new system you try, is moving you steadily in the right direction.

Be proud of yourself for every effort, even if it doesn't feel like enough. Daily successes or failures don't define your value. This challenging work of self-regulation deserves compassion. Each experiment and adjustment bring you closer to customised routines that nourish your well-being.

When motivation lags, recall why consistency matters - for your health, relationships, and life potential. You've got this. And if all else fails, adapt your standards today without guilt.

Tomorrow is a fresh opportunity to keep learning and trying again. You've overcome so much; a setback is a chance to advance differently.

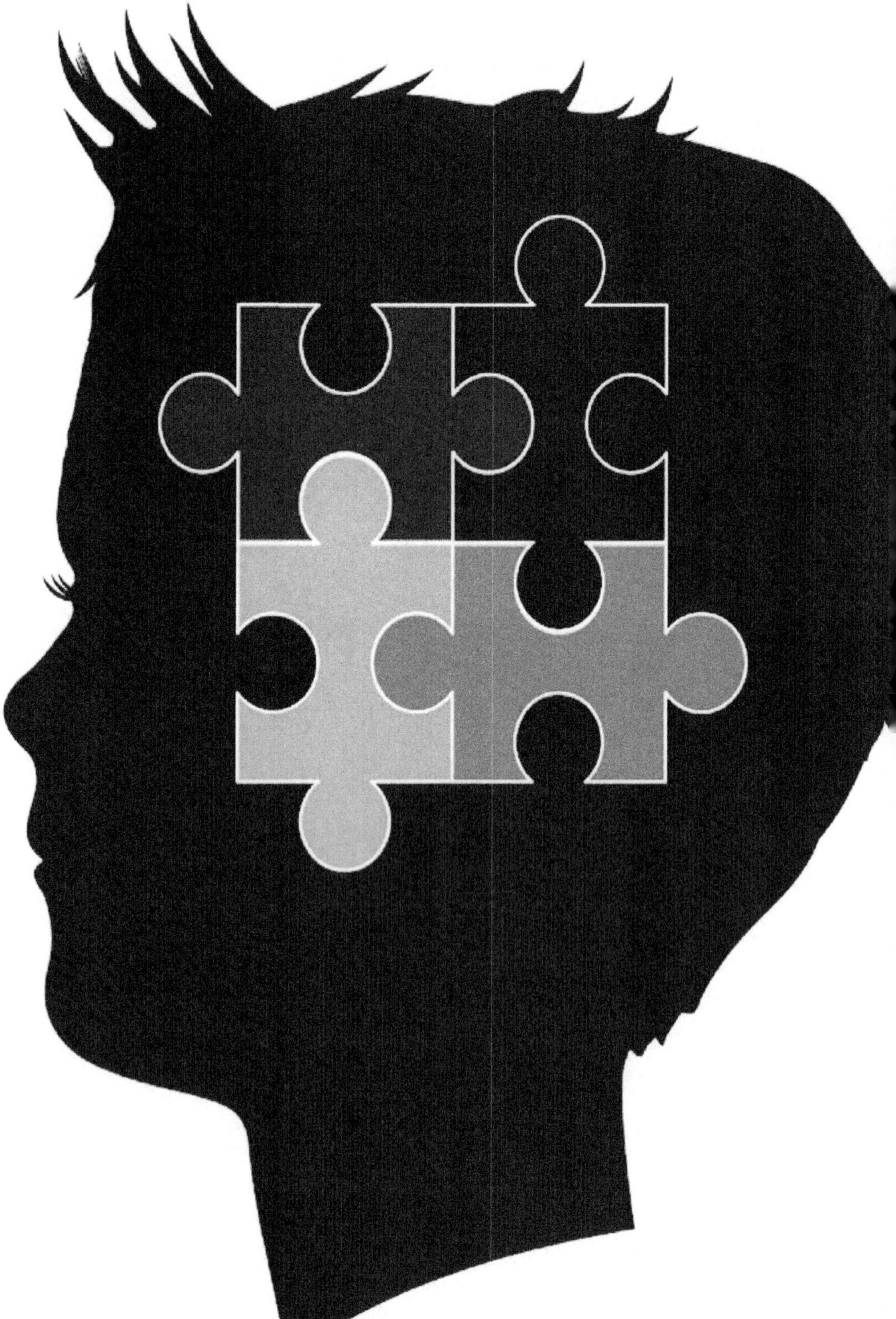

CHAPTER 11

Continuing Your Journey

Establishing effective routines provides many benefits, but maintaining them long-term requires ongoing effort and adaptation. This final chapter aims to inspire and equip you for the next phase of your journey as an ADHD survivor committed to daily discipline and growth. The strategies covered in earlier chapters have laid an essential foundation, but consistency occurs gradually through life experience. Consider what you've learned as an initial step toward cultivating lifelong habits and mindsets that serve your unique needs, priorities, and stages. Read on for guidance on nurturing routines and transforming them into an empowering, compassionate lifestyle beyond these pages alone. Your determination to thrive will see you through what challenges may come.

Looking back, seeing how far you've come in establishing daily routines and structures is incredible. Keeping an essential to-do list felt impossible when you began this journey. Now, you have optimised systems for planning your days, staying organised, managing chores and responsibilities, exercising regularly, and prioritising self-care. You can reflect fondly on pushing through many setbacks to reach this point where your routines feel empowering rather than draining. It reminds you how far consistency and a growth mindset can take you, even on the most challenging days.

As part of your continuous improvement process, you've learned so much from closely reviewing routines each month. Tracking habits have revealed patterns around what tasks or time frames derail your discipline the most. Changing routines has kept you feeling motivated rather than boxed in by rigidity. Combining different scheduling, organisational, and accountability methods has also proven highly effective for balancing responsibilities seamlessly with your unique needs, strengths, and lifestyle. Ultimately, a holistic approach to integrating daily routines as a supportive foundation for overall well-being has made consistency feel inspiring versus restrictive long-term.

Reaching this milestone wouldn't have been possible without resilience through many setbacks. Feel immense pride in how far your perseverance and willingness to learn from "mistakes" has brought you. With the routines and mindsets cultivated, you're empowered to seamlessly adapt this foundation to new phases of life, roles, and scenarios while ensuring self-care remains the priority. Your ADHD will undoubtedly present future challenges, yet this experience has given you profound confidence in your ability to rise above obstacles through patience, self-compassion, and continuous growth.

As you continue on your journey, it's essential to recognise that your needs, priorities, and understanding of ADHD will evolve. The routines that served you well during one season may need refinement as new responsibilities, stresses, or insights emerge. Regular self-reflection will help keep your routines dynamic instead of stagnant. Don't be afraid to experiment with changes as your situation changes. The knowledge and skills you've developed so far, like continuous tracking and change in habits, have prepared you well for this next customisation phase. With an open, learning mindset and compassion for yourself, you now have the toolbox to design schedules and practices that empower your unique experience of ADHD day by day, year after year.

Here are examples of how needs and routines may change and customisations someone could make:

If you have a child, meal planning and prep routines must be adjusted to accommodate less free time. Solutions could include doubling recipes for meal prep on weekends, using slower cooker meals, or providing partner support.

A new job with more travel may disrupt sleep schedules. Customising could involve relaxation rituals before bed, blackout curtains, and a travel routine/kit.

In university, study routines need to fit busier times. Solutions might be reserving library times, recording lectures, and minimising social media while working.

As relationships change, routines for connecting with others may need tweaking. Compromises could schedule regular one-on-one dates or keep in touch via short, frequent calls instead of long catching-up sessions.

If ADHD symptoms increase, current routines may require more structure or accountability. A personalised change could use calendar invites from loved ones to remember commitments.

Energy levels fluctuate with age. Simplifying routines, especially around hobbies or taking more restorative breaks, may help.

While your routines provide an essential foundation, continuing your personal growth also benefits from ongoing peer support. Seek local ADHD community groups and online forums to share experiences and encouragement with others facing similar challenges. Connecting with that community reminds you that you're not alone in your ADHD struggles and victories. It's also valuable to maintain check-ins with an ADHD coach or mental health professional to review routines and stress levels and make adjustments as needed with their expertise. Building rapport with an understanding healthcare provider ensures you have knowledgeable guidance available as needs change. Accessing occasional workshops or books on specific ADHD lifestyle topics freshens skills and mindsets. Foster a network of nonjudgmental family and friends to help keep you accountable and motivated. With continued community involvement, your wellness routine remains holistic and empowering.

Here are additional tips for ongoing support:

Join local Facebook groups to find ADHD peers in your area and start friendships and study groups.

Check if your university or workplace offers ADHD support programs with coaches and fellow professionals.

Go to conferences and meetups to meet inspiring ADHD activists and stay updated on best practices.

Consider an ADHD buddy to check weekly on routines and set shared goals and deadlines for accountability.

Set reminders to chat with your healthcare provider every 6-12 months to adjust medications.

Subscribe to ADHD podcasts and newsletters for new skills and stay motivated through others' stories.

Keep a journal to track symptoms, routines, and questions to discuss in therapy or with a life coach.

Use apps like "Coach. me" for on-demand reassurance and crowdsource routine feedback.

Ask family and friends to check stress levels and encourage regular catch-ups.

Be open about ADHD with loved ones so they understand setbacks and can celebrate wins with you.

Continued community involvement is critical to staying empowered on your ADHD wellness journey, as connecting with others facing similar challenges helps minimise stigma and isolation that can hinder progress. Sharing knowledge and resources with peers who understand the daily struggles provides accountability, motivation, and new coping strategies to try. When treatment methods aren't working as planned, others may have valuable alternative suggestions from their own experiences. Attending local ADHD meetups and continuing education courses keeps treatment-resistant issues from falling through the cracks, as symptoms may evolve, requiring change in wellness routines. Speaking at ADHD advocacy events or getting involved with related non-profits lets one pay forward the support received and elevate others beginning their treatment journeys, helping inspire confidence in managing one's condition. Online forums also provide 24/7 access to shared wisdom when motivation flags or a crisis requires immediate feedback, reducing isolation through virtual connections to augment in-person involvement. As relationships deepen from ongoing community participation, lasting friendships emerge with others accepting the neurodiversity within supportive accountability partnerships.

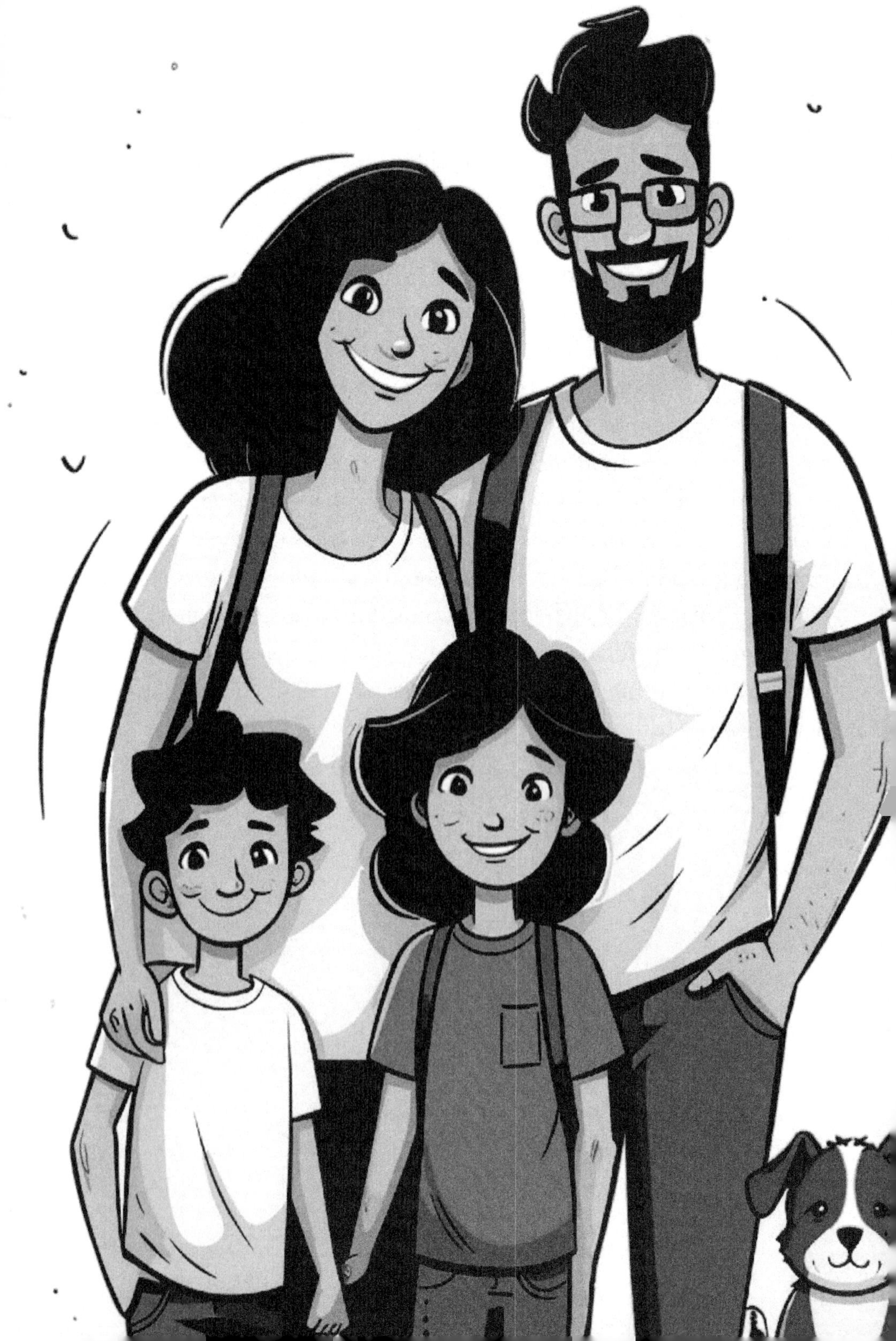

CHAPTER 12

The Family Impact of ADHD

While an ADHD diagnosis can bring a sense of relief in understanding the challenges experienced, it also often sparks a range of difficult emotions for both the individual and their family members. Feelings of fear, sadness, frustration and even guilt are common as loved ones process how ADHD may affect their dynamics and daily lives.

Parenting a child with ADHD introduces unique stresses and adjustments. From the hyperactivity and disobedience of early childhood to the organisational struggles and low self-esteem issues of the teen years, ADHD brings its own set of parenting hurdles that require patience, creativity and extra effort from mothers and fathers. Siblings also face challenges, like less attention from parents or feeling overshadowed by their sibling's needs. Supporting a child with ADHD can place immense pressure on relationships, communication styles and family routines.

Meanwhile, ADHD individuals confront self-doubt as they internalise perceived failures or conflicts with loved ones. They are navigating social settings with parents and developing independence while managing symptoms, which adds layers of complexity during development.

Unfortunately, many families find themselves ill-equipped to handle the subtle impacts of ADHD at home, which can breed resentment, enablement of poor behaviours or scapegoating over time if left unaddressed. Communication breakdowns may also occur if family members do not feel heard or make faulty assumptions about intentions and capacity.

This chapter aims to shed light on ADHD's far-reaching effects within a household by outlining common challenges families face. It provides evidence-based strategies and best practices for promoting open dialogue, establishing healthy routines, dividing household responsibilities fairly, and supporting all members in productive ways. With awareness, commitment and a tailored approach, families can weather the ups and downs that ADHD brings to the dynamic through unity and understanding.

The impact of ADHD is often most pronounced within the immediate family system. Whether it is a parent struggling with the difficulties of parenting a child with ADHD, siblings vying for attention or struggling with their adjustments or the individual with ADHD navigating challenges at home and internalising messages - the entire household feels the widespread effects in both subtle and real ways. On the surface, ADHD symptoms like hyperactivity, distractibility, disorganisation, and emotional volatility create obstacles to effective communication, consistent routines, and productivity. However, beneath are deeper undercurrents of mental health issues, role strain, fractured relationships, and damaged self-esteem that develop if household dynamics do not adapt to the unique needs created by living with this neurodevelopmental disorder. It is essential to understand how ADHD can ripple outwards from the diagnosed individual to influence family members so protective factors and support can be incorporated into daily life. Some of the most common challenges families confront include:

Disrupted Routines: ADHD can make maintaining consistent meal schedules, chores, and homework challenging. Transitions between activities are tough.

Sibling Favouritism/Resentment: Siblings may feel the child with ADHD gets more attention or leeway on rules, which can cause jealousy or acting out behaviours.

Parenting Stress: The additional hyperactivity, defiance, forgetfulness, or emotional dysregulation of ADHD can add significant stress to the parenting role. Over-correction is common.

Poor Communication: ADHD symptoms like interrupting, topic changes, and taking criticism personally can damage family interactions if left unaddressed long term.

Low Self-Esteem: Having ADHD symptoms leads to school/social struggles that negatively affect self-image development over time without support.

Financial Strain: Additional tutoring, treatments, organisational aids, and special school services required to support ADHD success add expenses for families.

Marriage/Relationship Tension: Caretaking roles can shift in unhealthy ways. Parenting frustrations may be taken out on each other without outlets.

Task Performance/Chores: Time blindness, lack of follow-through, and emotional meltdowns can frustrate expectations around shared family duties like cleaning, cooking and homework help.

Avoidance/Dependence: ADHD makes independent living skills like cooking and money management more difficult without direct tools. Enabling can occur.

Mental Health Issues: ADHD often co-occurs with depression/anxiety exacerbated by school/family stress if untreated.

Open communication is the cornerstone of any healthy family dynamic, but it takes even greater importance within families affected by ADHD. The neurodevelopmental differences and daily challenges brought about by ADHD can breed misunderstanding, unchecked frustrations or unintentional enabling behaviours if members cannot discuss concerns and feelings effectively. Left unaddressed over time, poor communication habits may escalate ordinary conflicts while the individual with ADHD receives mixed or invalidating messages about their worth and capacity. Regular family meetings that incorporate evidence-based relational techniques let misconceptions surface constructively, need to be clearly expressed from all perspectives, and united solutions formulated through compromise rather than resentment or subconscious favouritism. Respectful dialogue is crucial for families navigating the trial-and-error process of optimally supporting a member living with ADHD. Some best practices research indicates can help with more open exchanges include

Strategy 1

Set aside uninterrupted weekly time for check-ins without distractions like phones or TV. Ask open-ended questions to ensure all voices feel heard.

Strategy 2

Practise active listening. Make eye contact, rephrase what others said to confirm understanding, and avoid interruptions or solutions until they are finished speaking.

Strategy 3

Use "I feel" statements to share emotions without accusation and invite others to share feelings in a non-judgmental space.

Strategy 4

Compromise by finding middle-ground solutions through respectful discussion of all viewpoints rather than one person dictating decisions.

Strategy 5

Provide feedback respectfully by keeping it solution-oriented and specific rather than global criticism, which damages self-esteem and trust.

Strategy 6

Show empathy by trying to understand others' perspectives rather than having your own needs acknowledged. Validate others' emotions.

Strategy 7

Set ground rules as a family for hard conversations, like no yelling, blaming, or bringing up past arguments. Enforce these rules calmly in the moment.

Strategy 8

Seek family therapy if conflicts regularly arise from unresolved issues or unhealthy patterns like enabling. A mediator can help.

Strategy 9

Have routine check-ins about the ADHD treatment plan and adjustments needed from all members' input to keep a united approach.

While the symptoms of ADHD bring challenges, with understanding and teamwork, families can learn to thrive together.

However, creating an environment where all members feel heard, capable, and motivated requires forethought and consistency. Establishing clear, sustainable routines and equitably dividing household responsibilities are cornerstones of an organised, harmonious family unit navigating ADHD's daily impacts. When routines become unpredictable or specific individuals shoulder a disproportionate burden, resentment and pushback are expected outcomes. Families must put evidence-based strategies into practice to promote fairness, accountability, and interdependence amongst all members affected by ADHD - whether that be the individual with symptoms themselves, siblings, or parents. Fostering cooperation starts early by clearly communicating expectations and adjusting together as needs change.

Strategies for establishing healthy routines, dividing responsibilities, and supporting all family members include effective routines and equitable division of labour, essential for any household to function smoothly but take on even greater significance within families affected by ADHD. It is important to involve the entire family unit in creating clearly defined routines using concrete tools like written schedules, checklists, and calendars displayed in a common area. Tasks should be broken down into small, manageable steps to account for time management challenges. Responsibilities must also be divided according to each individual's unique strengths, limitations, age, and needs, ensuring no one feels overburdened. Assigning specific "jobs" can instil ownership, such as designating one person to manage weekly meal planning. The child with ADHD should have autonomy in allocating some of their duties to promote independence. Routines will inevitably require flexibility day to day as ADHD symptoms fluctuate, so punishment must be avoided and alternative strategies tried before reverting to consequences as a last resort. Acts of service and expressions of gratitude between family members can strengthen bonds of emotional support. Finally, prioritising regular enjoyable shared leisure activities each week, like game nights, movie dates, or story time, provides an outlet to decrease household tensions. With commitment from all parties to adapt routines through open communication and praise for efforts made, families can experience the benefits of cooperation instead of the pitfalls of imbalance or resentment when navigating daily life with ADHD.

While ADHD brings unwelcome challenges to family life, with understanding, empathy, and evidence-based strategies, its pervasive effects can be successfully mitigated. No household will have a flawless system, and flexibility will always be required as needs change throughout developmental stages. However, prioritising open communication, equitable distribution of roles based on each person's inherent worth rather than talents alone, and expressing gratitude regularly are foundational practices that promote unity instead of competition or bitterness. When all members feel respected for who they are and supported to reach their full capabilities through their unique neurodiversity, family bonds are strengthened. With continued dedication to adapting, problem-solving together, and embracing each person's intrinsic values, families can build a strong foundation of reliance, empathy, and care that lets the joys of shared life far outweigh its natural stresses.

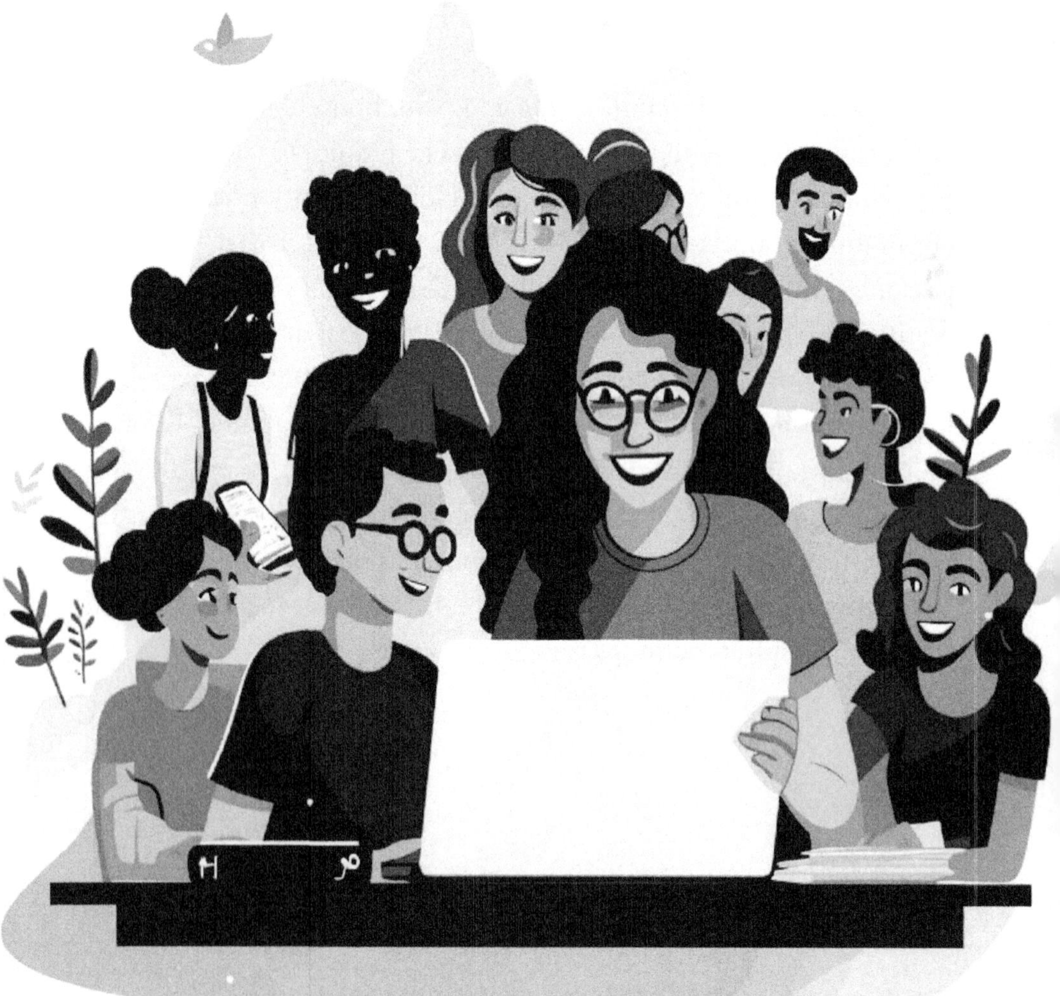

CHAPTER 13

ADHD and Social Interactions

For individuals living with attention deficit hyperactivity disorder (ADHD), navigating interpersonal relationships and social settings can feel challenging due to some of the disorder's core symptoms. Whether it's difficulties with regulating emotions, focusing in conversations, anticipating consequences of words or actions, or interpreting subtle social cues - ADHD traits have the potential to negatively affect everything from family and romantic bonds to workplace interactions and new friendships if left unaddressed.

However, having ADHD does not preclude someone from forming deep, lasting connections with others. Research shows people with ADHD have equal or greater capacities for empathy, loyalty, and intimacy compared to neurotypical peers, who face obstacles in the execution of specific social skills due to impairments in organisation, time management, flexibility, and working memory. Without proper support and strategy implementation, individuals with ADHD are also more vulnerable to issues like low self-esteem, rejection sensitivity, disruptive behaviours, and misunderstandings over intent that push people away.

This chapter aims to shed light on how ADHD's cognitive profile can manifest socially, both positively and negatively. It provides many practical techniques and mindfulness practices backed by science to help individuals with ADHD communicate effectively, establish boundaries, understand social/emotional cues better, enhance active listening skills, manage distractibility, and feel more confident engaging with others. With a commitment to learning and applying these evidence-based interpersonal tools, people with ADHD can meaningfully participate in relationships and leverage inherent strengths to build rewarding connections through self-awareness, honesty and compassion.

This chapter offers valuable strategies for navigating the intricacies of social dynamics. It intends to empower those with ADHD to overcome obstacles to fulfilling bonds and experience the therapeutic parts of healthy relationships.

Understanding how ADHD symptoms present in social contexts lays the groundwork for learning helpful strategies. The core cognitive impairments that define ADHD—such as inattention, hyperactivity, distractibility, poor working memory and emotional dysregulation—influence one's abilities in social interactions in both positive and negative ways. These differences may reflect personality or disinterest, but they stem from underlying neurobiological deficits that can be mitigated.

It is essential to acknowledge that ADHD does not preclude people from enjoying fulfilling relationships or forming solid bonds. Instead, the disorder may require some accommodation and alternative approaches compared to neurotypical social development. With self-awareness and proper support, individuals with ADHD can easily emphasise their inherent interpersonal strengths and minimise weaknesses with foresight and planning.

Understanding how ADHD's cognitive profile manifests in social performance provides a launching point for understanding one's unique challenges and learning tools to overcome them. Some ways symptoms commonly influence social skills include both potential positive and negative impacts on parts like attention, hyperactivity, distractibility and more. By examining these effects in greater detail, one can start identifying personal patterns and areas for growth.

Here is how ADHD's cognitive profile can manifest socially, both positively and negatively:

Positively:

Impulsivity and risk-taking can manifest as charm, spontaneity and adventure-seeking in social interactions.

Hyperfocus allows intense listening and interest when engaged, making for lively conversations on passionate topics.

External stimulation, rather than words, enhances attention to social cues like body language and emotion.

"Big picture" thinking style excels at unconventional problem-solving and group thinking outside the box.

Negatively:

Inattention makes it hard to follow conversation threads and societal "rules" like eye contact or taking turns.

Distractibility causes missing social/emotional cues or interrupting due to outside stimuli.

Being hyperactive or fidgety may cause discomfort for others unaccustomed to high activity levels.

Poor working memory impacts the ability to monitor personal performance socially and remember names.

Dysregulated emotions could result in disproportionately intense reactions or outbursts.

Deficits in the organisation make planning social events or keeping in contact with peers difficult.

Mastering social interactions does not come naturally for many with ADHD, but aiming to improve is an achievable and impactful goal. This section outlines evidence-based strategies shown to enhance communication abilities, strengthen boundaries, boost self-esteem around others, and allow neurodiverse minds to participate fully in relationships. With a commitment to learning and implementing these tools tailored to individual needs, people with ADHD gain insights into their style while developing interpersonal skills for lifelong benefit.

Some techniques and mindfulness practices that can aid effective communication include active listening strategies like making eye contact, restating key points, and avoiding distractions; mentally rehearsing conversations to prepare for various topics and emotional responses; writing out an overview or agenda to stay on track; and taking turns speaking without interrupting. Establishing boundaries helps to set limits respectfully but firmly, say "no" when overwhelmed, and remove oneself from draining social situations without guilt. Understanding social cues can be strengthened by analysing facial expressions and body language cues in photos of emotions. Managing distractibility involves identifying internal and external triggers and then using grounding techniques such as deep breathing, fidget toys, or changing environments when triggered. Listening to affirming self-talk and recognising inherent social strengths build confidence to engage positively with others.

While social interactions can present unique challenges for those with ADHD, building practical skills in critical areas lays the foundation for greater confidence and success in relationships. Many individuals on the neurodiverse spectrum struggle with issues like difficulty maintaining appropriate personal boundaries, detecting and interpreting subtle social cues, focusing during conversations, managing external distractions, and feeling secure interacting with others. However, research shows these obstacles respond to targeted strategies and mindfulness practices. Learning evidence-based techniques tailored to ADHD traits empowers individuals to overcome social hurdles through awareness, preparation and self-acceptance. This section provides many tools proven to help establish boundaries, understand social dynamics, listening skills, distractibility management and boost self-assurance when engaging with people. With practice and commitment to continually developing interpersonal skills, individuals can experience rewarding personal connections.

Establishing Boundaries

Say "no" respectfully when overwhelmed. Remove yourself from overstimulating situations without excuses. Be clear about what you can/can't commit to.

Understanding Social Cues

Study photos showing facial expressions/body language cueing various emotions. Watch social situations and try labelling what you observe. Replay interactions are analysing missed cues.

Active Listening

Maintain eye contact intermittently. Paraphrase what's said to ensure understanding. Limit distractions by avoiding phones/side conversations. Ask open-ended follow-up questions.

Managing Distractibility

Identify internal triggers (hungry, tired, stressed) and external triggers (loud noises, busy visuals). Use fidgets or grounding techniques (deep breathing, stretching) when attention slips. Ask for white noise or music in some settings.

Confidence Building

Track social strengths and give yourself credit. Challenge negative self-talk with rational thoughts. Surround yourself with supportive people who appreciate you. Join ADHD peer support groups.

Mindfulness Practices

Guided meditation focuses attention. Noting emotions/thoughts boosts self-awareness. Gratitude journaling highlights social wins. Yoga links breathing with movement to relieve tension.

While social interactions may at first seem challenging for those navigating neurodiversity, this chapter illuminates how individuals with ADHD have an immense capacity to meaningfully engage with others through cultivating key skill sets. With a dedication to self-reflection, implementation of practical strategies, and compassion for the complex nature of human relationships, people on the ADHD spectrum control their destiny when forming bonds. While the journey requires ongoing effort, each step builds resiliency, community, and a deeper appreciation for neurotypical and neurodiverse perspectives. With insights gained here and perseverance and support may all individuals find empowerment to participate confidently in relationships that nurture authenticity, personal growth, and joy. Remember - by recognising strengths, practising skills learned, and extending patience to oneself and others, fulfilling connections are well within reach.

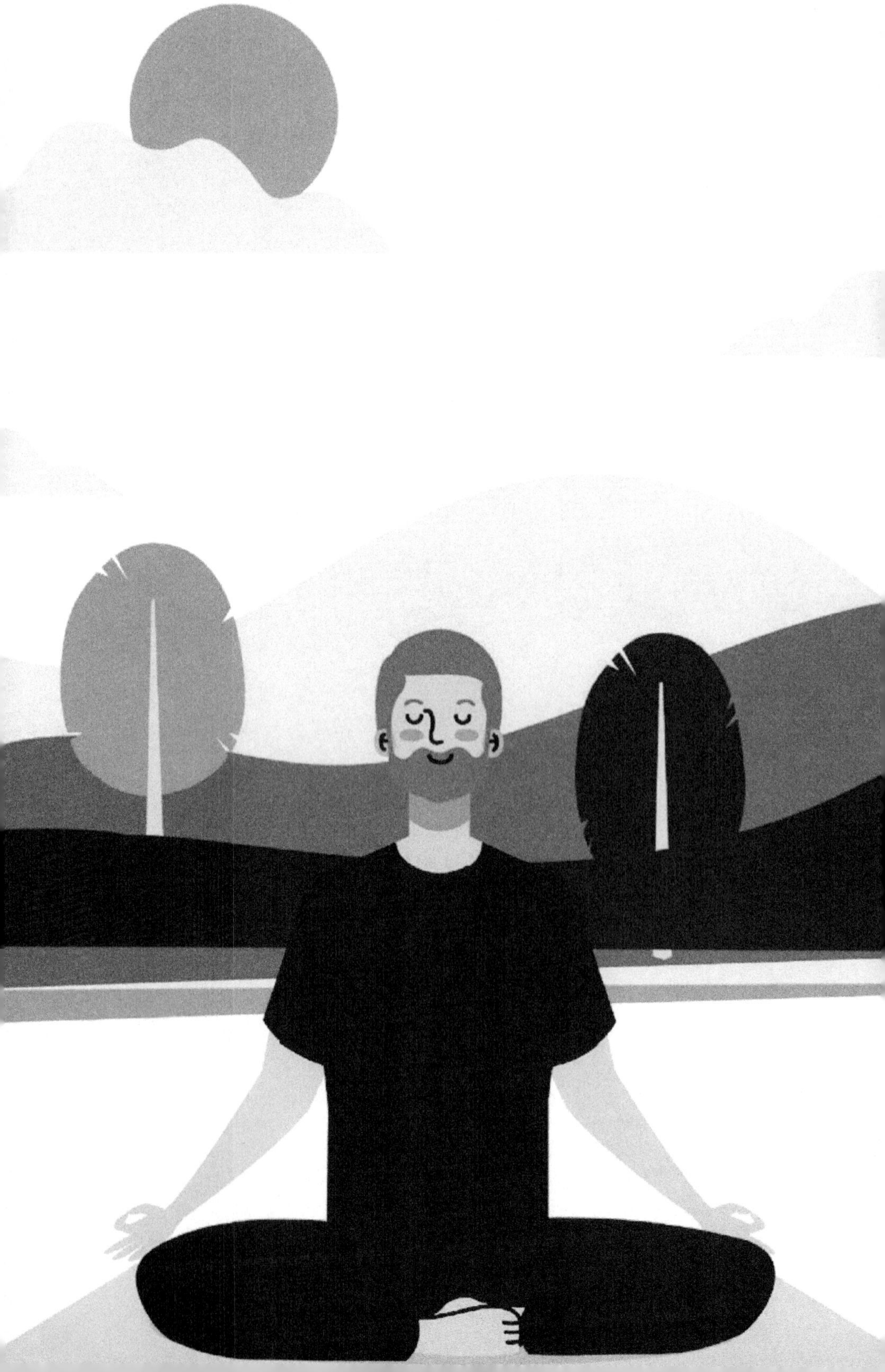

CHAPTER 14

Health and ADHD

While medication plays an important role in treating ADHD symptoms pharmacologically, lifestyle factors also significantly influence one's daily experience with the disorder. Recent research has increasingly highlighted the mind-body connection, showing how we eat, how active we are, and the quality of our sleep and downtime directly affect cognitive functioning, mood regulation, and overall mental well-being. For those with ADHD, optimising nutritional intake, exercise habits, sleep hygiene, and stress management may offer natural, complementary strategies for supporting symptom control.

This chapter aims to provide an in-depth exploration of various lifestyle components that research shows can help manage the core challenges of ADHD when practised consistently as part of a holistic self-care routine. Specific dietary and nutritional factors like caffeine consumption, meal timing, and essential macronutrients and micronutrients will be examined for their effects. The chapter also digs into how physical activity, relaxation techniques, prioritising restorative sleep, minimising blue-light exposure before bed, and establishing daily rhythms can all lend mental clarity and focus. The roles of mindfulness, meditation, journaling, and seeking social support networks will also be discussed.

By learning actionable lifestyle changes grounded in science, individuals will gain powerful non-pharmacological tools to ease troublesome ADHD traits. Committing to small, sustainable changes can improve well-being, concentration, productivity, and quality of life. An integrated approach considering medical and lifestyle aspects has substantial potential to aid comprehensive symptom control.

While medication plays an important role in ADHD treatment, lifestyle choices also significantly affect one's experience with the disorder daily. Recent research increasingly highlights the mind-body connection - what we eat, how we move, sleep, and relax all directly influence cognitive functioning, mood regulation, and well-being. For those with ADHD, optimising these lifestyle components offers natural, complementary strategies to medication for managing core challenges.

Diet

Omega-3s (fatty fish, flax, chia) have anti-inflammatory properties and support dopamine & norepinephrine production. Aim for 1-2 grams per day.

Protein is important for sustaining attention throughout the day. Choose lean meats, eggs, nuts/seeds, and legumes. Space protein intake evenly between meals and snacks.

Hydration improves blood flow and nutrient delivery to brain cells. Drink half your body weight in ounces of water daily. Carry a water bottle.

Limit added sugar, refined carbs & caffeine, which spike blood sugar & release cortisol/adrenaline, exacerbating hyperactivity & emotional dysregulation. Instead, focus on complex carbs and fibre.

Exercise

Aerobic exercise for at least 30 minutes daily, thrice weekly, improves prefrontal cortex efficiency through increased blood flow and neuroplasticity. Walking, jogging, and cycling are easily incorporated.

Strength training 2x weekly strengthens motor skills & provides an outlet for physical energy. Free weights, resistance bands or bodyweight exercises at home.

Sleep

Routine is important - same bedtime & wake windows daily, including weekends, normalising circadian rhythm.

Cool, dark environment & technology curfew 1 hr. before bed avoid blue light blocking melatonin production.

Track duration & quality - most need 8-10 hours, but needs vary; aim for consistency.

Stress management

Mindfulness meditation - Training attention and impulsivity through daily practice.

Relaxation techniques - Deep breathing, progressive muscle relaxation, and yoga to reduce anxiety.

Manage time/responsibilities - Feeling rushed or overwhelmed exacerbates executive dysfunction.

While eating patterns, macronutrients, and meal timing are important considerations for managing ADHD symptoms through diet, particular foods and nutrients warrant focused discussion. Zeroing in on specific dietary components allows a deeper understanding of their direct impacts on brain chemistry and functioning.

This section aims to unpack research surrounding important nutritional factors that significantly influence cognitive processes challenged by ADHD, like executive function, concentration, and impulse control. Caffeine consumption, hydration levels, fibre intake, and many essential vitamins and minerals will be examined given their roles in supporting or hindering mental clarity and regulation.

With ADHD affecting dopamine and norepinephrine pathways in the brain, it makes sense that the fuel we provide through our plates also matters. Individual dietary tweaks have meaningful potential to complement other treatment modalities. While consistency is critical, minor changes can be tested to observe any benefits or drawbacks for personal symptom presentation.

With targeted knowledge of specific nutritional compounds, readers can consider dietary optimisations that better serve their brain health needs. Let's explore caffeine, meal spacing, macronutrient makeup, and important vitamins and minerals to reveal how targeted nutrition may naturally support ADHD challenges.

Caffeine Consumption

Recommend limit of ≤200mg per day (1-2 cups of coffee)

Sources: Coffee, tea, energy drinks, chocolate

Effects of overconsumption: anxiety, irritability, disrupted sleep, decreased focus, increased hyperactivity

Tips: Track intake, limit after lunch, and find caffeine-free alternatives like tea.

Meal Timing

Benefits of breakfast: stabilised blood sugar and focus throughout the morning

Recommend 2-3 meals and 1-2 snacks spaced 3-4 hours apart

Impact of skipping/delaying meals: blood sugar crashes, irritability, fatigue Sample schedule: Breakfast 8 am, Lunch noon, Snack 3 pm, Dinner 6 pm

Macronutrients

Protein: 0.8g/kg body weight daily, found in meat, eggs, dairy, legumes, nuts Carbs: Complex over simple for stable energy, examples of whole grains, starchy veggies

Fats: Emphasise omegas from fatty fish and nuts, and aim for 2-3g EPA+DHA daily

Fibre

Foods: Whole grains, fruits, veggies, and legumes help digestion and regulate appetite

Recommended intake: Women 25g, Men 38g daily

Vitamins/Minerals

Vit D: Regulates neurotransmitters synthesised from sun exposure & foods like salmon

B vitamins: Support brain energy production, found in meat, eggs, bananas, potatoes

Iron: Transports oxygen, lean meat, lentils, and spinach; pregnancy can deplete levels

Zinc: Supports brain development/function, shellfish, seeds, nuts

Magnesium: Calms nerves and relaxes muscles, leafy greens, nuts, and seeds, limit supplements

Hydration

Daily needs: Around 64 oz or eight glasses for women, 96 oz or 12 glasses for men

Signs of dehydration: Thirst, dry mouth, headache, fatigue, irritability

Tips: Water bottle with time reminders, flavour additives, limit caffeinated/sugary drinks

While diet and nutrition play an essential role in ADHD management, lifestyle habits equally affect one's daily experience with the disorder. Recent research increasingly highlights the connection between physical and mental well-being. Our exercise routines, relaxation, sleep, and rhythm setting influence cognitive processes like focus, impulse control, and stress levels.

This section will explore evidence-based lifestyle strategies shown to complement ADHD treatment. Physical activity, relaxation techniques, prioritising restorative sleep, minimising blue-light exposure before bed, and establishing daily rhythms can all lend mental clarity and focus when practised consistently. Attention to holistic wellness through optimised routines offers natural, complementary approaches to medication.

The demands of ADHD symptoms like hyperactivity, distractibility, and dysregulation create cumulative stress. However, implementing health-promoting habits empowers individuals by relieving pressure sustainably. Making minor changes with a commitment to self-care strongly supports symptom management. Let's examine specific lifestyle factors with the potential to ease executive dysfunction challenges through dedicated rest and restoration for the body and mind.

Physical Activity

Aerobic exercise boosts dopamine, and norepinephrine improves executive function and focus.

Recommend 30+ minutes daily of walking, running, sports, dance, etc.

Strength training 2-3 times/week releases stress hormones and provides outlet

Relaxation Techniques

Deep breathing for reducing stress and anxiety

Progressive muscle relaxation helps shift out of the fight or flight response

Guided imagery and meditation lower cortisol and heart rate for mental calm

Restorative Sleep

Optimal 7-9 hours per night for adults

Develop a relaxing bedtime routine without screens

Keep screens out of the bedroom or use the blue light filter after sunset

Establish a consistent wake/sleep schedule daily

Daily Rhythms

Regular schedule stabilises circadian rhythm and internal body clock

Try to eat, exercise, and wind down at consistent times

Minimise late-night eating, screen time, or stimulants before bed

Exposure to morning sunlight supports mood and focus

While lifestyle and nutrition play important roles in ADHD management, mental wellness strategies also provide natural relief from distressing symptoms. The demands of this neurodevelopmental disorder invite accumulated stress when left unaddressed. However, implementing mind-body practices empowers individuals to ease physiological and emotional pressure sustainably. This section will explore evidence-based techniques to nurture focus, relaxation, and emotional processing abilities challenged by ADHD. Mindfulness, meditation, journaling, and seeking social support networks cultivate strengths within the prefrontal cortex and limbic system. Even brief daily practice of these strategies can have significant cumulative benefits for reducing anxiety and boosting focus and self-awareness.

Mind-management skills empower individuals to disengage from fixating thought patterns and regulate overwhelming feelings in high-stress moments. When committed consistently, they strengthen neurological responses to challenges. Let's examine specific practices with the potential to complement ADHD treatments through dedicated cultivation of attentional control and emotional balance. Holistic lifestyle interventions offer natural paths to symptom relief and personal growth.

Mindfulness

Focused, non-judgemental present moment awareness of thoughts/sensations

Techniques like body scans and breathing exercises cultivate attentional control

Meditation

Sitting practices like meditation lower the stress hormone cortisol and quiet mental chatter

Apps/videos provide guided meditations for beginners to do 5-10 min daily

Journaling

Writing down thoughts/feelings freely without editing helps organise the mind

Journaling about stressors provides emotional release and perspective Journal prompts help focus thought exploration on growth areas

Social Support

Connection with others buffers stress and encourages a sense of belonging Support groups and communities specifically for those with ADHD uplift through shared understanding

Expressing feelings openly to trusted loved ones lifts the emotional burden.

Successfully managing ADHD involves a balanced whole-person approach. While medication is essential, complementary strategies through optimised diet, routine-building, physical activity, and stress relief naturally support core deficits. When committed consistently, minor sustainable changes in many areas have the potential for meaningful cumulative impacts on symptoms. Empowerment comes through education on evidence-based practices and finding what modalities resonate personally. Continue experimenting to discover optimised wellness routines that lift the burden of this disorder. Remember that effective self-care nurtures both body and mind alike. Stay determined while also staying compassionate toward yourself as you move forward in your ADHD journey.

Conclusion

This book covers much important information about ADHD — from the latest neuroscientific understanding of its causes to practical, evidence-based strategies that can be implemented daily. The goal has been to give you a comprehensive yet accessible overview of ADHD so you can take control of your journey through continued learning and self-management.

In going through this material, some main conclusions can be drawn:

ADHD is a valid neurological difference with actual impairments, not a personal weakness or excuse. Understanding its biological basis through brain imaging research can help reduce stigma.

There are multiple presentations of ADHD beyond stereotypes, and severity exists on a spectrum. Recognising nuances is essential for tailored support.

Strategies must be personalised to your strengths, challenges, and lifestyle using tools grounded in neuroplasticity principles. What works may differ at each stage of life.

Mindset affects the ability to manage ADHD long-term. Replace any notion of limitations with empowering philosophies like a growth mindset focused on learning from challenges.

ADHD does not define your skills or potential - you have the agency to apply solutions creatively and continuously optimise your effectiveness. Community helps sustain motivation.

This resource aims to educate, inspire and empower readers in their self-advocacy journey. Refer back to gain new insights, refresh on methods, or look up related articles for specific situations. Connect with others experiencing similar challenges. Keep refining personalised techniques over time based on iterative testing. Be compassionate and celebrate yourself for continued efforts towards progress, not perfection. I hope readers take away an enlightened sense of control over ADHD through a lifelong dedication to growth.

You've got this! No matter how small, every step of progress moves you closer to your goals. Believe in yourself and your ability to build on your strengths.

Remember - adversity introduces us to ourselves. Every challenge you face makes you wiser and builds your resilience. Keep your head held high.

Reflect on how far you've come when the path ahead seems unclear, paused or turbulent. Each experience, both joyous and challenging, has shaped you into the person you are today. Feel empowered by your journey.

Your beautifully unique mind is capable of so much. This book is the beginning - keep unlocking your potential by learning, adapting and celebrating small victories each day. You've got this!

Author's Note

We have now reached the end of our journey together through this guide to understanding and taking control of ADHD. When you first picked up this book, you were probably overwhelmed by the challenges of navigating daily life with this condition. However, I hope the insights and strategies shared have helped empower you to see ADHD in a new light - not as a set of limitations but as an opportunity to cultivate your strengths.

While the road ahead may not always be easy, my goal in writing this book was to arm you with practical tools based on scientific research, customised approaches, and a growth mindset framework to help you overcome any obstacles that might arise.

Remember that having ADHD does not define your potential for success, happiness, and fulfilment - it is simply one part of your life that makes you who you are.

This profound neurodevelopmental difference gives you a unique perspective and way of seeing the world. Now equipped with the knowledge of how your brain works, mindfulness techniques, organisational systems, and support networks, I know that you have the power to live on your terms.

Though the journey of self-management is lifelong, each small victory of persevering through challenges and putting strategies into practice to optimise your strengths will lead you closer to your goals.

You have so much incredible potential to offer the world. I hope the lessons in this book help nourish your self-belief and motivation to keep learning and adapting your toolkit.

Though we may face setbacks, embracing difficulties with compassion empowers continuous growth. With dedication and support, there are no limits to what you can achieve.

You've got this - now go out there and shine! I wish you all the best in your ADHD journey. Stay curious, be kind to yourself, and remember that simply doing your best each day is enough. All the best!

Templates

Now that we've explored various evidence-based strategies for taking control of your ADHD, it's time to provide customisable templates to help with the application. Templates are helpful tools that reinforce strategy by making them tangible and actionable. The templates in this section are designed to be interactive and adapted to your individual needs and daily routines. They cover areas like planning your schedule, setting goals, tracking focus sessions, journaling thoughts, and tracking habits. Don't feel restricted by these examples - change them in any way that best supports your workflow. The aim is to equip you with practical reinforcement of concepts discussed while allowing flexibility. With practice and tweaking over time, templates can foster productive routines to optimise your effectiveness. Choose the templates most pertinent to your current challenges and goals, try them, and learn through experimenting with customised formats.

Daily Planning Template

Time	Task/Appointment	Notes
8:00-9:00 AM	Make breakfast, pack lunch	Set the alarm for 7:30 AM
9:00-10:00 AM	Work on homework assignments	Prioritise the most challenging subject
10:00-11:00 AM	Meet with a study group	Remember notebook and textbooks
11:00 AM 12:00 PM	Lecture	Sit at the front and review notes after
12:00-1:00 PM	Eat lunch, take a break	Plan healthy dishes for the week
1:00-2:00 PM	Gym class	Remember to bring gym clothes
2:00-3:00 PM	Tutoring session	Bring specific questions prepared
3:00-4:00 PM	Downtime	Read recreationally or do a hobby
4:00-5:00 PM	Start dinner	Involve family in cooking activity
5:00-6:00 PM	Free time	Be mindful of screen time limits
6:00-7:00 PM	Homework, chores	Schedule challenging assignments first
7:00-8:00 PM	Family time	Plan fun board games or movie night

Weekly Goals Template

Priority Area	Goal	Deadline
Academic	Finish history essay draft	Friday by 5 PM
Health	Go to yoga 3 times	Track in planner
Social	Contact old friends	Send two messages by Tuesday
Household	Do laundry twice	Wednesday and Sunday
Hobby	Practice guitar for 30 min daily	Track practice times
Self-Care	Go for a walk after dinner daily	Note in journal
Finance	Stick to a budget for groceries	Weekly grocery trip on Saturday

Pomodoro Timer Template

Use the Pomodoro Technique and this template to maximise your focus time:

Task: _____

Pomodoro #1

Focus Time: [ ] - [ ]
Break Time: [ ] - [ ]

Pomodoro #2

Focus Time: [ ] - [ ]
Break Time: [ ] - [ ]

Pomodoro #3

Focus Time: [ ] - [ ]
Break Time: [ ] - [ ]

Pomodoro #4

Focus Time: [ ] - [ ]
Break Time: [ ] - [ ] How did it go? What can be improved?

_____ _____

Brain Dump Journal

Use this template to write down anything without judgment to declutter your brain freely. This lets you let thoughts flow instead of worrying about structure.

Date: _____

8:00 am:

9:00 am:

10:00 am:

11:00 am:

Noon:

1:00 pm:

2:00 pm:

3:00 pm:

4:00 pm:

5:00 pm:

6:00 pm:

7:00 pm:

8:00 pm:

Habit Tracker Template

Use this template to track your progress with developing new habits or breaking old patterns. Track your performance to gain insight and stay accountable.

Habit: _____

Week 1	Week 2	Week 3	Week 4

Habit: _____

Week 1	Week 2	Week 3	Week 4

Habit: _____

Week 1	Week 2	Week 3	Week 4

Notes:

The templates in this section are meant to serve as a starting point for putting the strategies discussed in this book into action in a personalised way. Using the templates, you can build routines to manage tasks, focus periods, goals, thoughts, and habits in a structured yet adaptable manner. This helps turn methods into maintained practices. The templates also let you monitor their progress, spot patterns, and identify areas for improvement. Over time, subtle changes to the templates based on lessons learned can further optimise their effectiveness.

In addition, templates promote accountability by creating clear plans and records of performance. This keeps you on track to achieve goals while also keeping the management of ADHD on top of your mind. Perhaps most important, the templates empower you by placing control and creativity in their hands. They can and should be remixed as needed to suit best changing schedules, environments, and phases of focus/motivation. Rather than becoming rigid dictates, the templates cultivate flexibility, which is so essential for the lifelong management of ADHD. With regular use and revision of templates tailored to their lives, you can develop sustainable systems that work harmoniously with your neurodiversity to help them reach their fullest potential.

References

American Psychiatric Association. (2013). Diagnostic and statistical manual of mental disorders (5th ed.).

https://doi.org/10.1176/appi.books.9780890425596

Dweck, C. S. (2006). Mindset: The new psychology of success. Random House.

Erickson, R. (n.d.). ADHD quotes. ADDitude.

https://www.additudemag.com/adhd-quotes/

Huberman, A. [AndrewHuberman]. (2023, January 17). Dopamine and ADHD: How low levels impact focus and motivation [Video].

YouTube. https://www.youtube.com/watch?v=hnOPu0taX-4
Huberman, A. (2023). Your brain is making you procrastinate: The dopamine experiment [YouTube channel].

https://www.youtube.com/c/AndrewHubermanLab/videos

Barkley, R. A. (1997). Behavioural inhibition sustained attention, and executive functions: Constructing a unifying theory of ADHD. Psychological Bulletin, 121(1), 65–94. https://doi.org/10.1037/00332909.121.1.65

Biederman, J., & Faraone, S. V. (2005). Attention-deficit hyperactivity disorder. Lancet, 366(9481), 237–248.

https://doi.org/10.1016/S0140-6736(05)66915-2

Castellanos, F. X., Sonuga-Barke, E. J., Milham, M. P., & Tannock, R. (2006). Characterising cognition in ADHD: Beyond executive dysfunction. Trends in Cognitive Sciences, 10(3), 117–123. https://doi.org/10.1016/j.tics.2006.01.011

Faraone, S. V., & Biederman, J. (2005). What is the prevalence of adult ADHD? Results of a population screen of 966 adults. Journal of Attention Disorders, 9(2), 384–391.

https://doi.org/10.1177/1087054705281478

Kessler, R. C., Adler, L., Barkley, R., Biederman, J., Conners, C. K., Demler, O., Faraone, S. V., Greenhill, L. L., Howes, M. J., Secnik, K., Spencer, T., Ustun, T. B., Walters, E. E., & Zaslavsky, A. M. (2006). The prevalence and correlates of adult ADHD in the United States: Results from the national comorbidity survey replication. American Journal of Psychiatry, 163(4), 716–723.

https://doi.org/10.1176/appi.ajp.163.4.716

Willcutt, E. G. (2012). The prevalence of DSM-IV attention deficit/hyperactivity disorder: A meta-analytic review.

Neurotherapeutics, 9(3), 490–499. https://doi.org/10.1007/s13311012-0135-8

Printed in Great Britain
by Amazon